BEING IN
STEP
WITH
GOD

Rick Schin

WESTBOW
PRESS®
A DIVISION OF THOMAS NELSON
& ZONDERVAN

WestBow Press books may be ordered through booksellers or by contacting:

WestBow Press
A Division of Thomas Nelson & Zondervan
1663 Liberty Drive
Bloomington, IN 47403
www.westbowpress.com
844-714-3454

ISBN: 978-1-6642-4156-5 (sc)
ISBN: 978-1-6642-4155-8 (hc)
ISBN: 978-1-6642-4157-2 (e)

Library of Congress Control Number: 2021915262

Print information available on the last page.

WestBow Press rev. date: 8/18/2021

This book is dedicated to the memory of my loving parents, William and Marie Schin. They were always supportive of my efforts in life.

CONTENTS

PREFACE

"In the Beginning ..." "Fun to be around ... Member of CC's track team ... Faithful choir member ... Little League coach" was what appeared beneath my name in my high school yearbook in 1967. This is what was written about me, because no one really *knew* me! That's right. The yearbook staff passed around a fact sheet, which I filled out myself. Someone was supposed to interview us students, but at least in my case that didn't happen. Even though no one would believe it now, I was a very shy, introverted boy unless I knew you well.

My shyness—actually, the term *wallflower* would be more accurate— was only worsened by my wearing black chino pants, white socks, and black, pointy shoes topped off by my slicked-back hairstyle. All the other guys were wearing wing-tip shoes and variously colored socks. Their pants were cuffed, and their hairstyles were the barely combed look—easy maintenance, if you know what I mean. I had to use a lot of Brylcreem to keep my hairstyle look. You know: "A little dab'll do ya."

The story begins in Queens, New York City. The year doesn't matter. One month before I turned sixteen (August 1965—*oops*, do the math), we moved to Camp Hill, Pennsylvania. Other than my immediate family, I knew only one person who lived down the street from me. Benny (not his real name) and I had only met once before, because our fathers worked together and they'd visited us once in New York.

When we lived in New York, from about the age of eight, my family and I went to a Protestant church just down the block from our house. It was kind of cool to be able to walk to church when the weatherman made it possible for us to do so. Even in Queens I went to Sunday school and church almost every week. I sang in the choir and participated in church plays.

Yes, we were regular churchgoers, but people's faith stories weren't talked about the way people did in PA. "Turning your heart over to Christ" was never a phrase that I'd ever heard spoken in the church in Queens. Pastor Brown used to preach about "making a commitment" to God, but I do not recall him giving an invitation from the pulpit to follow Christ.

I thought of myself as basically being a good kid. I was a member of the church, but I hadn't accepted Jesus into my heart. A funny Queens, New York story: I was always seeking a personal, *real* relationship with God. As a young boy, my Sunday school teacher showed us film strips about how God had audibly spoken to various Bible characters. I thought, *How amazing would it be to have God speak to me out loud!* One evening, before choir rehearsal, I went into the sanctuary to pray. I sat there and I prayed something like "Lord, if You are real, please speak to me out loud like You did with the Bible-times people." All at once I heard, *"Are you planning to be in here much longer?"* It scared me half to death! It was the janitor getting ready to clean the carpets in the sanctuary. Wild, right?

There were no major changes when we moved to Pennsylvania. Our family quickly found a church, Dad and I joined the choir, and we got involved in Sunday school. We seemed to easily make friends and began to fit in at our new church.

A short time later, we discovered that the move would change the entire course of our lives. I accepted Jesus into my life at a Billy Graham movie being shown in Hershey, Pennsylvania. The title of the picture was *The Restless Ones.* The story involved young people who were members of a motorcycle gang. Though I had never even ridden a motorcycle, let alone been involved in *a motorcycle gang,* I received the message of salvation anyway. At the conclusion of the movie, an invitation was given to accept Jesus Christ as my personal Savior. I made a commitment to Christ at the front of the theater that day. When I opened my eyes, standing right beside me was my dad. He had also accepted Christ that day. What a marvelous, treasured memory. That was step one in creating the foundation for the rest of this book—but more importantly for the rest of my life! I have been so grateful for the ministry of that amazing preacher and person, the late Rev. Dr. Billy Graham.

Reflection: Is there someone you might identify with as having had a significantly positive influence in your life as you've developed into the person you've become?

ACKNOWLEDGMENTS

_____

I very much appreciate those who took the time to read partial manuscripts and gave me their unbiased and truthful, constructive, critical opinions. Recognizing God first and then my family and friends has made this book whatever it has turned out to be. *Thank you all!*

INTRODUCTION

This book is a collection of scripture passages, personal stories, and other narratives explaining how believing in God and Jesus Christ and acknowledging the presence of the Holy Spirit can provide a formula for a successful life. It is my belief that within these pages you will find nuggets of encouragement that will help you expand the horizons of your life. What I have written about is *real*. I have been exercising and putting my faith into practice for quite some time. There aren't any gimmicks in here, just applications that when adopted will help you grow in your Christian faith, realizing that with God's help you can follow and live a Bible-guided life.

I am delighted that you have decided to pick this book up. Now read, enjoy, and find out what *Being in Step with God* is really about!

BELONGING TO CHRIST

In 2 Corinthians 5:17 (NLT), the apostle Paul writes, "Anyone who belongs to Christ has become a new person. The old life is gone; a new life has begun!" Even though I probably hadn't been aware of Paul's writing at the time I accepted Christ, I know I witnessed the reality of Paul's words. I *did* feel something. I wasn't the same kid! My desire to tell others about the *new me* was strong. I recall a school bus ride the Monday morning after my conversion weekend. I sat next to Clay Watson (not his real name). I was feeling bold that morning. I was a *new person!* The love of Jesus was in my heart! There was a conversation that most likely started with "So what kind of a weekend did you have?" Please understand Clay and I had almost nothing in common. I rode the bus with him to school, but he was not from my neighborhood, we were in different academic programs, and we just didn't see much of each other. I can't remember what his weekend was like, but I surely knew what had happened to me over that weekend! I proceeded to tell Clay about *The Restless Ones*, the story involving kids who were part of a motorcycle gang. Then the fact that I had *accepted Jesus Christ as my personal Savior* came spilling out of my mouth! I wasn't ashamed to tell Clay that I was a new person and that he could accept Jesus Christ into *his* life too!

The next thing that happened could've easily killed any chances of me witnessing about my faith ever again! Truth be known, I've never forgotten the moment, and I still hesitate sometimes to tell others about my faith in Jesus Christ. Clay looked at me and said, "Man, Rick, I never heard you swear before!" Wow, what a letdown, right? I can't be certain as to what I said after that, but it was apparent to me that Clay had no idea who Jesus was. The only way Clay had ever heard of the name of Jesus Christ was when that name was used as a curse word. There's a lyric from a gospel

1

song I once heard about how Christ is not supposed to be used as a swear word. Christ is the Son of God.

I *was* a new person. To tell you that I never sinned again after committing myself to following Jesus would be a lie. My growth in the Lord has been an uneven rise and drop, a series of hills and valleys. If I were to try to diagram my personal growth pattern, it would probably look like a heart monitor with ebbs and flows, ups and downs. I've heard it said, "Christians aren't perfect. They're just forgiven."

Paul continued in 2 Corinthians 5:18–19 (NKJV). "God … reconciled us to Himself through Jesus Christ and has given us the ministry of reconciliation: that God was in Christ reconciling the world to Himself, not imputing their trespasses to them. And has committed to us the word of reconciliation."

Reconciliation may be defined as "to make one account consistent with another, especially by allowing for transactions begun but not yet completed" (https://www.lexico.com/en/definition/reconcile). For accountants, being able to reconcile accounts is the main focus of their profession. If the numbers don't add up, if the cashier's cash drawer doesn't "hit" at the end of the day, someone will need to provide an explanation. Paul wrote that "God … reconciled us to himself through Christ" (2 Corinthians 5:19 NKJV). God has always looked to have a strong relationship with His people, beginning with the Hebrew nation of the Old Testament. Throughout history, people have disappointed and turned their backs on God. But as surely as people have disappointed God, God has never given up on people! "God … reconciled us to himself through Christ" (2 Corinthians 5:19 NKJV). God sent Jesus to earth *to make one account consistent with another, especially by allowing for transactions begun but not yet completed*. For us to be made right, or consistent with the desires of God, Jesus Christ had to take the burden of our sinful nature upon Himself. Christ was the perfect sacrifice for our sins—so that we might receive eternal life in heaven. "Allowing for transactions begun but not yet completed," realize that humans are an experiment in progress. God needs to repeat the reconciliation process many times over. "He has committed to us the message of reconciliation" (2 Corinthians 5:18 NIV). With God's help, we can reconcile other people with ourselves. And we should live in a spirit of reconciliation toward others. It seems the older I grow, the more interested I am in accomplishing this task. I can tell you that should you want to do the same, your efforts will not be successful without the help of Jesus.

Reflection: Is there someone in your life who has had a major impact in your life as you've grown and matured? Has something gone wrong and the two of you need to have the relationship reconciled?

WHO CARES ABOUT ME? GOD CARES

Matthew 10:29–30, 6:33; Psalm 55:22.

"Cast your cares on the Lord and he will sustain you; he will never let the righteous fall" (Psalm 55:22 NIV). "Not one sparrow ... can fall to the ground without your Father knowing it. And the very hairs of your head are numbered" (Matthew 10:29–30 TLB). I am reminded of the balding man who described his monthly trips to the barber shop as "a search and destroy mission." He remarked, "I pay the barber a finder's fee. He doesn't get paid to *cut* my hair. He is paid to *find them!*" The older I get, the more I can identify with that statement.

It would be wise to stay close to God, considering the various insurance programs in this country carrying annual premiums totaling approximately $460 billion. The words from the gospel of Matthew and King David's psalm make traveling with the Holy Spirit our best course in life.

Depending on the season, the stresses and strains in your life can take their toll. Accepting Christ as your Savior will not *exempt* you from experiencing life's problems. Following Jesus's teachings provides the way to *endure* and *overcome* life's difficult circumstances.

It's exciting to know that when I am confronted with the rigors of life, even if no one else wants to listen to me, I *know* that I can go to the Lord Jesus, and He will certainly hear me. How awesome is that? As an aside, I think the word *awesome* is incorrectly and overused by people today. But you'll have to understand I've spent seventeen years teaching teens and preteens. The word *awesome* is given to explain anything from

4

the amount of eyeliner a girl uses to a viewing of the moon shot from the 1960s. The definition of *awesome* is "inspiring an overwhelming feeling of reverence, admiration, an overwhelming feeling of reverence, admiration" (Dictionary.com).

For God to care that "not one sparrow can fall to the ground without [the] Father knowing it" really *is* awesome (Matthew 10:29 TLB)! The authors of the Living Bible estimate that a sparrow, during the time of Matthew's writing, sold for "two for a penny" (Matthew 10:29 TLB). In other words, certainly depending on the income of a person, most likely everyone would have been able to afford buying one or two sparrows. Yet even at this meager price, your Father in heaven knows if one sparrow falls, maybe out of a nest in a tree. That's (my favorite word) awesome! So should you be going through a particularly low time in your life when the events of the world make you wonder whether anyone cares, *stop!* Stop and recall Matthew 10:29. "Not one sparrow can fall to the ground without your Father [yes, your Father in heaven] knowing it" (Matthew 10:29 TLB). Another teen expression: that's cool!

King David, having had his own issues in life, says, "Cast your cares on the Lord and He will sustain you; He will never let the righteous fall" (Psalm 55:22 NIV). "Give your burdens to the Lord. He will carry them. He will not permit the godly to slip or fall" (Psalm 55:22 TLB). Are you asking, "How do I get to be one of the godly people the king was referring to?" That's simple. Ask Christ into your life! There are no magic words, no incantations, and no prerequisites. You go to the Lord in prayer, and ask Him to come into your heart. A *salvation prayer* is included later in this book.

The more advanced in age we get—I know, you're saying, "You mean the older we become, right?" Let me start over. The older we become, the more physically challenging life seems to be. As the stages of your life seem to influence your decision-making, it's very possible that you could begin to weaken, ask *why*, and become discouraged and maybe even disgusted. I'm here to say don't! Don't do it! Don't become discouraged. Don't get disgusted!

"Cast your cares on the Lord and he will sustain you; he will never let the righteous fall" (Psalm 55:22 NIV). There's the good news of the gospel—the good news of Christ for His followers. "Not one sparrow can fall to the ground without your Father knowing it. And the very hairs of your head are numbered" (Matthew 10:29–30 TLB). We joked about "the very hairs of your head [being] numbered," but let's just pause a bit here and try to let that sink in. "The very hairs of your head are numbered" (Matthew 10:29–30 TLB). I think I know what you're thinking. "I can't even wrap my brain around *that* concept." I know, right? Well, I realize that I'm the one writing this book, but what God *does* and *how He does it* are two different things.

Let me explain. I believe what the Bible says—100 percent! I know that if God said it, it's so. I am willing to *eliminate nothing*. I don't have to know *how* God *does* what He does. I accept much of my Christianity by faith. I hope that I won't lose your respect on this. For those intellectuals, for the scientists potentially reading this book, I am sorry if you stop reading at this point. Let me just reiterate that I have experienced many marvels that have happened throughout my walk with Christ. I can't explain them, but everything I have written regarding my experiences is genuine and has taken place. Believe it!

Reflection: Are you at a point in your life *right now* where you're feeling like no one cares very much about you and your situation and you don't matter? Please reread this section, take your cares to the Lord, and then seek out a solid Christian friend or acquaintance to share and pray with.

CHURCH—REALLY?

"The world's sin is that it refuses to believe in me" (John 16:9 NLT). In the Sunday, November 24, 2019, edition of the Harrisburg, Pennsylvania, *Patriot-News,* there was an article entitled, "Leaving behind Church … and Community." The subtitle was "Changing Philosophy: As More Millennials Skip Worship Services, We Lose the Glue That Helps Our Towns and Neighborhoods Stick Together." The article announced that millennials had "stopped going to church." Based on 2017 data taken from the American Time Use Survey, millennials have "stepped back dramatically from religious activities." Millennials are working more and spending their free time on the internet and social media. Involvement in a church translates to the development of deeper, longer-lasting relationships—a physical, live, sit-down-next-to *community.*

Community is a group of people living in the same place or having a particular characteristic in common (Google.com/searchcommunity). Millennials might respond, "Yeah, like Facebook, Instagram, Twitter, LinkedIn, etc. I get it! Community!" With all due respect, a person doesn't even have to get out of his PJs-with-the-feet-in-'em to do *that* form of community. Now I'm not completely left in the Stone Age. I'm on Facebook and moderately follow the FB activity. I enjoy seeing what others—my "friends"—are up to with their lives. Possibly I might even confess that I do believe I would miss this connecting tool if I didn't use it. I will tell you that I recently gave up Facebook as a sacrifice during the Lenten season. I found it not to be a major sacrifice. However, I was glad when I could get back to checking FB activity after Easter.

Social media is like any other communication medium. It can be used for great things, or not! It certainly has been proven to literally lead to the death of some members of our society. As a schoolteacher, I saw how the introduction of social media can be a wicked way for mean-spirited students to bully others just for sport. I was bullied at school as a child. But at the end of the school day, when I went back to my neighborhood, I was able to reconnect with my friends to escape the bullies at school. Today, no thanks to social media, students are unable to escape or resist the taunting of the school bullies in their lives! We have all read about those cases in which the bullies' victims have even taken their own lives just to escape the tormenters.

"Leaving behind church and community" is no small thing. Social media will never adequately replace "community." The community of believers in Christ—Christ followers—are those people who will be by your side during the highs and lows of your life. They should not be underestimated or undeservedly minimized. There have been many times in my life when life itself seemed dismal at best. Whether it was the loss of employment, being passed over for a promotion, or when I needed to have a triple-bypass heart operation, my community of believers was there to support me with their prayers and other well wishes. I knew they were praying. I *felt* their prayers for me! There are few better feelings than knowing that your brothers and sisters in Christ are asking God for blessings on your behalf. OK, millennials, the social media community can do that too. Touché. I'm down with that.

The age-old religious question has been "Can a person be a Christian and not go to church?" In other words, what if a person is an invalid and not ambulatory—a shut-in (how's that for a "churchy" expression?)—and cannot *get* to church? I get it! Well, it's been my experience that very often *the church comes to them*. That's right! Church members or the pastor will visit or call them to keep them included. But you have to have initially made the connection for this practice to become a reality in your life.

"The world's sin is that it *refuses* to believe in me" (italics added; John 16:9 NLT). Jesus's words are compelling! Many of today's millennials are committing the very sin spoken of by Christ in the book of John. For me, as I reflect on the last eighteen years of my working career, having invested myself in the lives of approximately 2,000 students and having met many of the parents and siblings of these children, I am saddened by the prospect of these wonderful people committing such a costly sin. Refusing to believe in Jesus doesn't just mean not going to church. Refusing to believe in Jesus impacts your eternity! Jesus Christ made the ultimate sacrifice for all who will claim Him as Lord of their lives! Jesus wants to have an intimate, eternal relationship with you and me and all who believe in Him. Paul writes, "If you confess with your mouth the Lord Jesus and believe in your heart that God has raised Him from the dead, you will be saved. For with the heart one believes unto righteousness, and with the mouth confession is made unto salvation" (Romans 10:9–10 NKJV). Right now, if you do not know Jesus Christ as your personal Savior, right where you are, please pray this salvation prayer:

Dear Jesus,

I know I'm a sinner and don't deserve to receive Your forgiveness. I understand that You are forgiving me of my sins and that Your sacrifice on the cross was payment for the many sins I have committed and will commit in the future. I know that You took the punishment for the wrongs I have committed. Thank You for not giving me what I *deserve*. You saved me from being condemned for my sins so that I can spend eternity in heaven with You. Thank You, Jesus. *Right now*, I accept Your *free gift of salvation*. Please come into my heart and save me from my sins.

Thank You, Jesus.
Amen.

If you've just prayed this prayer, please understand that the first step toward eternal life with God has been accomplished. The next step you should take is to walk into a church the very next Sunday and begin to worship as a new believer! "How do I find a 'good church'?" you ask. You might ask a churchgoing neighbor or even a coworker if you might go to church with them. The point is you need to begin to develop a devotion— putting your faith into practice as soon as possible. You will begin growing your faith in Christ and developing a relationship with Him.

"The world's sin is that it *refuses* to believe in me" (italics added; John 16:9 NLT). If you are a millennial—or anyone else for that matter—I beg you to break the mold that is being cast. Look to develop strong Christian relationships. Find a church, and become part of that community of believers. I am sure that you will be received well by a church filled with people who are truly committed to following Christ. I can tell you that there isn't a church on earth where there are no glitches. When selecting a place to worship, look for the Word of God to be preached from the pulpit every Sunday. Do not expect there to be a zero tolerance for un-Christianlike behavior. Trust me. I haven't discovered a place where this is being pulled off. You know why this happens? Every church is filled with (hello!) human beings! Wherever you house human beings, it will be inevitable that there will be un-Christlike behavior at times. If the pastor is preaching from the Bible and not just his or her opinions on current events, you might decide to settle in that church. I've heard it said that if you find the "perfect church" —you know, the church where there are no hypocrites or otherwise sinful people—-do not join. Get out! You'll only mess it up!

So first, accept Christ's free gift of salvation. Then find a Bible-believing church where the Word of God is spoken from the pulpit every Sunday. Lastly, enjoy living the life of a Christ follower who travels in the good company of the Holy Spirit. Glory to God!

Reflection: Have you prayed the salvation prayer and you're looking for the *next step* so that you'll be able to grow in this new life as a Christ follower? You've taken the first and most important step: accepting Christ's free gift of salvation. Now find a Bible-believing church where the Word of God is spoken from the pulpit every Sunday.

PRAYER: THE IMPACT IT CAN HAVE ON YOUR LIFE

The apostle Paul writes, "Devote yourselves to prayer, being watchful and thankful" (Colossians 4:2 NIV). A former, now deceased, pastor of mine, D. Rayborn Higgins, once preached a sermon and cautioned the congregation against praying selfishly, saying, "Gimme, gimme, gimme; my name's Jimmy." Prayer is often misinterpreted by many people.

When we pray, God should not be looked upon as some type of supernatural personal promoter who goes about granting people's wishes. God is not a genie. God is the ruler of the universe! We should subscribe to a method for looking beyond a wish list before the ruler of the universe. My prayer times have typically been invested in going to the Lord as a go-between intervening for others. This is known as intercessory prayer. I make my prayers conversational, leaving out the old-fashioned thee's and thou's often confused by many who perhaps do not really understand praying. These people may be limited to a "Now I lay me down to sleep ..." type of prayer life. In my devoted, deep-prayer time, I invite the Holy Spirit to commune with me right there in my personal space. It can be very powerful to set up a certain time and place for disciplined prayer and Bible study every day. By doing this, a person will mature in his or her prayer life, and meaningful prayer will be the result.

For the most part, I have not kept my prayer practice a secret. What is really awesome is that when people hear and discover that you pray, they will share their lives with you, asking for prayer for their needs. Offering to pray for the needs of others has provided me another entre into being a witness to my faith. I recall an acquaintance of mine calling me one day very stressed out. She said, "Rick, I know that you pray. I am at the hospital in the emergency room. Will you please pray for my child?" I prayed with her over the phone. Prayer in a time of need such as this can have a calming effect for the one asking for the prayers. There is little that can be more rewarding for a prayer warrior than to have someone contact you in this way. *"I know that you pray"* becomes what your ministry and mission in life is about.

Paul instructs his readers to be *devoted to prayer.* Those who are *devoted* to *anything* need to be *all in*, *sold out*, and *fully committed* to their belief in it. For me, prayer has become second nature. I thank Jesus for so many things daily. For example, when I first entered my classroom each day, clicked on the remote to my electronic Smart Board, and *it worked,* I thanked Jesus that the remote control was working and the tuner was receiving the appropriate signal. The unit that needed tuning was at the ceiling and if malfunctioning, I needed a ladder or a tall student with a yardstick to adjust it to make it functional. It was with this electronic tool that we viewed the announcements of the day, as well as using it as another teaching tool. This is why I thanked God *every morning* that it was working properly.

Making your relationship with Christ more reachable, more genuine, and *more real* involves regularly communicating with Christ through the Person of the Holy Spirit. The Holy Spirit can be *real* if you will recognize the presence of His Spirit. Short, one-word or simple-sentence-prayers believed, but not always communicated aloud, will give you the realization that the Holy Spirit *is with* you and of comfort where and when you need the Spirit.

Prayer has been an important resource in my walk with Christ for a long time. I think it became so because of a prayer-warrior model: my late mother. Yes, Ethel Marie (Schaefer) Schin really prayed, *a lot*. Mom would retire in the evening to another room and pray. She was conscientious and sincere about her prayer time. I am sure she remembered our family, and then she would probably pray for people at work, church, and others she may have heard were facing life's experiences and were in need of blessings from God.

Both my parents were believers and committed to prayer, although my father took a more functional viewpoint. My dad would use prayers very regularly and easily in his everyday undertakings. I imagine this is where I may have formed my opinions about seeing prayer as a tool for tapping into the Holy Spirit. Prayer is a resource for everyday living in the presence of the Holy Spirit. Dad might have been working in the garden and finding himself unable to put his hands on a tool that he needed. As he would unsuccessfully look everywhere he thought the tool could be, he would finally *stop and ask God* to find the tool for him. Of course, the tool would appear to have been right there all the time, but being a faithful Christian pragmatist, I am convinced that God placed it for him where he eventually found it.

Unlike my father, rather than waiting until I am unable to find something or looking for help, I pray *immediately*, requesting the help of the Holy Spirit. Before marking me down as being truly stark-raving mad, the next time you can't find something, especially something of great value or importance, pray that God will show you where the object is. My experience tells me that you will find it.

I have tried to learn from both my parents. There is a routine for my prayer time. I inherited that from my mother. For years, as I was getting up for work or teaching school very early in the morning, I would read the Bible and a short devotional piece. Then I would pray about my list of prayer needs and requests. My prayer list began as people would tell me of the situations in their lives, and I would tell them, "I'll remember you in my prayers," only to simply forget to do so. I decided to write down the requests, but the list grew too long to easily manage. Since then, the list has expanded to include many individuals with assorted requests. My prayers are need driven. Because I have made my prayer ministry known, the prayer list has been arranged according to the requests that have been shared with me. I list individuals and then regularly pray for them. The list includes healings for cancer, matters I have called "other healings," personal needs, prayers for our country, and general needs. I pray for those who are mourning. Matthew 5:4 (NAS) reads, "Blessed are those who mourn, for they shall be comforted." This is one of God's promises, and it should not be overlooked. For these folks, my prayer is that they will *recognize and realize their blessing from God* and *be comforted*. Praying through the scriptures in this way pleases God and keeps us familiar with God's Word. In Isaiah 55:11 (NKJV), the prophet writes, "So shall my word be that goeth forth out of my mouth: it shall not return unto me void, but it shall accomplish that which I please, and it shall prosper [in the thing] whereto I sent it." Making note of the date of the death, I pray for exactly one year about those who mourn. It was very difficult for me to adjust during the first year of grieving after my mother passed away.

The power of prayer and the fact that someone knows there are those praying is significant. While I was in the hospital during my heart surgery, I *knew* I was being prayed for, and it was definitely a contributor to my successful healing.

You see, I have been so blessed by my solid, faithful, caring, and supportive parents. I can't imagine trying to live my life without the presence of the Holy Spirit making my life so much easier—watching over and giving me a type of *safety net* throughout my life. I'd say once again, "Don't knock it unless you've tried it."

Having been a schoolteacher for eighteen years, I always made it known that I didn't go to school without first having prayed each morning. My day would start somewhere between 4:00 and 4:30 each morning. When asked, "Why so early?" I would normally explain that I had the usual tasks in the morning, and then I had quiet time and prayer before breakfast and making my lunch for later in the day.

One time, my principal told a Latin teacher assigned to our building to come and talk with me about managing my classroom with a particularly hard-to-reach student. The man said, "I am going to be having this girl next semester, and the principal tells me you know how to handle her." I said, "OK, first of all, understand that I don't come to school without first praying." His response to that was "Oh, OK …" Unfortunately for this teacher, the conversation ended there. He didn't stick around long enough to hear where my strategies went from there.

So I start each day with prayer. I don't believe there is any right or wrong way to pray. Almost twenty years ago, I was introduced to The Prayer of Jabez. This prayer is highlighted in the Holy Bible in the book of Chronicles, chapter 4, verses 9 and 10. Jabez was a well-respected man, an ancestor in the kings' lineage of the tribe of Judah.

I pray this prayer daily for myself, and I pray this over members of my family as well.

Oh, that you would bless me indeed, and enlarge my territory; that Your Hand would be with me, and that you would keep me from evil, that I may not cause pain. (1 Chronicles 4:9–10 NKJV)

There is an amazing spiritual lift to using this prayer each morning. It's almost like getting a kick start and putting your mind in the right space. It's like receiving a spiritual lift.

Reflection: Have you begun to pray more often, and are you sensing God's closeness like what we've written about in this section?

GRACE IN YOUR LIFE—
GIVING AND RECEIVING

Along with my praying The Prayer of Jabez, I've added the following to my prayers each day. "Oh, that you would place *your riches of grace* into my life's account. I dare not and I do not wish to squander them" (ref. Ephesians 2:7–8 NIV).

Probably the thing *most* needed and *least* activated in all qualities of life in the world today is a small, five-letter word: *grace*. Every human being needs grace, but so little of it finds its way into the human experience. We are so quick to criticize, even if we don't really know all the facts. We can't seem to let others have their space. Society seems to strive and thrive on getting everyone else to be just like us. And we aren't shy about letting the other guy know that *we want to be correct*—we *want to be right*. If we can't be right, then we'll move into argument territory. My mother-in-law has an interesting take on the need to be right. When in a potentially confrontational conversation, she says, "If you know you're right, there's no reason to argue. If you're *wrong*, you *shouldn't be* arguing, because *you're wrong!* So you see, there should never be an argument." The idea here is that arguments happen, because people feel the need to have their viewpoints *validated* by the others in discussions.

Let me just tell you I have used my mother-in-law's technique often. Watching the reaction of those arguing is worth the effort. When the discussion is obviously not leading to a positive resolution, you simply say, "That's OK. I'm good. No problem," and you either walk away satisfied or just stay and go on to the next topic. The other persons just don't even know what to do about that. Often they still want to discuss the subject.

But their heads are *ready to explode*, because *they need validation! They have to have you confirm that they are right!* Walking away from this unofficial contest doesn't make you look weak; it elevates you to the level where you are basically saying, "My relationship with you is more important to me than your agreement with me at this time." We live in highly charged times. Politics and religion are topics that creep their way into our lives—usually at the Thanksgiving Day dinner table or on a summer night's chat on the patio. Confirmation of one's point should not become a wedge between loved ones or neighbors. By using my mother-in-law's technique, you are showing that elusive five-letter word—*grace*—and providing all parties an escape route that will honor and preserve important relationships.

Wouldn't it be terrific if the world would listen to my mother-in-law and conduct themselves accordingly? By the way, every son-in-law should be as fortunate as I have been to have a mother-in-law like mine!

"Oh, that you would place *your riches of grace* into my life's account" (ref. Ephesians 2:7–8 NIV). As a former banker, I have invested a lot of my time gaining experience talking to people about their accounts (investments). When I talk about "my life's account," I am reminded of the accounts people opened and maintained with the banks where I worked.

What if we were to consider God's "riches of grace" as something people could accumulate—maybe like deposits into a "grace account" to be available when the need for grace situations arise? Certainly, everyone most likely has been in need of grace, either from God or others. We are all in need of grace. As Christians, we know that we've all sinned and fall short of the glory of God, which is why we all need grace. The apostle Paul writes in Romans,

> Righteousness from God comes through faith in Jesus Christ to all who believe. There is no difference, for all have sinned and fall short of the glory of God, and are justified freely by His grace through the redemption that came by Christ Jesus. (Romans 3:22–24 NIV)

For a Christian, this means that she is looking to stay in a right relationship with God, and the only way this can be accomplished is through the grace of God. We cannot meet God's standards of living on our own. Our faith in Jesus's sacrifice on the cross for our sins and God's grace will keep us blameless.

All are "justified freely by His grace through the redemption that came by Christ Jesus" (Romans 3:22–24 NIV). "Justified …" Hmmm. Being justified is like when a jury in a court of law finds the defendant "not guilty" and he gets to go free, to never be tried again for the same offense. What Christ did for His followers on the cross was to save believers from eternal damnation. As a Christian, you're certainly not *innocent* regarding the crime of sinning! No! "For all have sinned and fall short of the glory of God" (Romans 3:23 NIV). We know that! So also know that Christ's sacrifice on the cross, the grace that He places on our heads, declares us "not guilty" of our many sins. Glory and gratefulness to God!

Grace is something that is sought by those who find themselves in life's situations—sickness, a death in the family, or a difficult relationship—that are either actually or potentially disruptions or devastating occurrences, and they need a touch of grace to see them through. I believe that my prayer is a way of storing up God's riches of grace, and I don't want to take God's grace lightly. I want to have something to fall back on when my life is lacking—for better health, for financial stability, or because of the loss of a loved one. Just as if I found the need to make a monetary withdrawal, if I needed to go to God for a "grace withdrawal," I pray that God's "riches of grace" would be there in *my life's account.*

Be it while driving a car, having to wait for an attendant in a fast-food restaurant, or forgiving a spouse, parent, or child, we can all identify with times in our lives when situations required us to show grace to others. These are times when showing grace to the person should come easily and automatically, because surely Christ has shown us *His grace.* But sadly, from personal experience, I don't always model grace-like behaviors.

Consider how important and valuable God's grace is. Staying with the idea of depositing grace into an account, with my daily prayer, I am asking God to help me not squander or lose these grace riches that God blesses me with. "Oh, that you would place your riches of grace into my life's account. I dare not and I do not wish to squander them" (ref. Ephesians 2:7–8 NIV). I dare not "squander them" for me is a healthy reminder of the overwhelming, undeserved, and unmerited love and grace given to me by God. He forgives and forgets my foibles—no, my sin! When I need God's grace, the *distribution of blessings*, I want to be in a position whereby the channels are open between God and me. Don't misunderstand. I know that if I am feeling estranged from or not close to the Lord, it isn't *He who moved*; it is I. I get that! My daily prayer is for *my benefit*. I want to stay intentionally close to Him.

Let's consider another aspect of acquiring and perhaps storing up "riches of grace," where people could accumulate "shares"—maybe like deposits into a "grace account." They could be available when the need-to-display-grace situations arise. A person would have "riches of grace" available to them to "invest" when coming in contact with those people who might frustrate us and take us either out of character or even show a side of our natural character we intentionally attempt to avoid. You know what I mean. You're not "feeling yourself" or someone cuts you off along the highway, and your humanity gets in the way of your witness. The dilemma is the old question of *how Jesus would handle this* opportunity. It would be so valuable to invest or spend some of the grace riches you've hopefully stored up in order to save some face and not ruin anyone's day. There needs to be a degree of *stewardship* with grace, much like how we develop and cultivate with our finances. Doling grace throughout our interactions with others could do wonders for our kingdom building. It will draw others to the saving grace of Jesus Christ. You see, God, Christ, and His Holy Spirit are placing the "riches of grace" into our lives' (grace) accounts. We need to look to spending or investing these riches. Scripture tells us to not store up treasures here on earth (Matthew 6:19 TLB) but to be generous, giving them away. Just imagine what life would be like if instead of getting upset—annoyed, snapping at others (especially those we love and are closest to us)—we would be pleasing to them and treating them with love and kindness. What if we were gracious toward them, making them feel as special as so many times we know they are to us? The world should be able to identify us as being Christ followers being *different* from the rest of the world, because of the grace we are prone to move toward, demonstrate, and shower others with!

There was a radio talk-show personality in the Harrisburg, Pennsylvania, market who used to say, while in the middle of a heated discussion with a caller, "Give me a physical break!" Haven't we all felt this way at some point in our lives? "Give me a break!" And God did, and does, repeatedly, doesn't

He? Christ gave us not only *a break*, but Christ also promised us a new life—*eternal life with Him!* When we accept Christ's ultimate sacrifice on the cross, we are on the path to heaven and eternity without pain, fighting, or darkness. We are saved from the agony of eternal damnation.

Grace isn't always easy to put into practice. Grace is a factor in daily living that gives us the greatest opportunity to practice our faith. I wish I could tell you that spreading grace all over the landscape is something we can develop and that I have become a real champion in so doing. *Not!* Here's a story to demonstrate the point. One of the more active churches in our area puts on a Christmas drama every year. Some of our family, myself included, have participated in these performances over the years. Well, this one year, while awaiting the start of the show, my ability to show grace was really put to the test. Because it was the "friends and family" performance, it's the final dress rehearsal performance before the real thing, we had to scramble to get good seats. As fate would have it, a family with four or five children under the age of eight sat behind us. To make matters worse, for me anyway, the parental supervision of these children was barely present. The parents were letting these kids do whatever they pleased. As an old-time educator and parent, I was *losing my mind!* The kids were not only unruly, but they also began kicking the back of my seat. Not just once but fairly consistently, and then a couple of them began hanging onto the back of the seat, thrusting themselves into the air space of our row. So anyone who knows me can just imagine what was going on in my head. We had our granddaughter sitting with us. She was behaving the way "good children" *should* act when going to see a play. (No, really, she was doing so well!) In my head, I had played out all the possible scenarios should this behavior have continued once the play started. As an aside, my dad used to say that his mother-in-law, my Nana was good at planning interactions with her sometimes confrontational siblings. You know … *well, when he says this, I'll tell him … and when she says that, I'll say …* and so forth. Well, my Nana, would have been proud of me. I was doing the same thing. One of my concerns was any inadvertent physical interaction among the kids and my young granddaughter. So just imagine the turmoil going on in my spirit. I am a pretty strict disciplinarian, so with all this random, chaotic activity behind me, I felt like I was going to lose it at any time! In Psalm

103:8 (NIV), we read, "The Lord is compassionate and gracious, slow to anger, abounding in love."

To be honest, I can't be certain that I remembered this scripture word for word, but the Lord may have prompted me to do what I did. I prayed, "Please, God, help me to show grace." The result of that prayer was to have the male adult (I think he was a father, an uncle, or even perhaps an older brother) separate the children, placing them among the adults so that there was better supervision and less chaotic behavior during the show. The kicking of the seat ceased, or at least lessened. Even though I had had my speech ready to go, where I obviously would have potentially started something among the adults, my prayer, God's intervening, and showing grace saved the moment. We enjoyed the show.

In Luke 17:11–17, we read about Jesus's healing of ten men who were suffering from a dreaded disease of that era: leprosy. Ten men approached Jesus and asked Him to heal them. For many reasons, not the most basic of which was a lack of education concerning this malady, the practice was that if someone diagnosed with diseases was rid of the disease, he needed to report to or present himself to a priest. The priest would declare him clean (Leviticus 14:1–7 TLB). In Luke 17:14 (NIV), Jesus tells the men, "Go, show yourselves to the priests." Luke 17:15 (NIV) reports, "When he saw he was healed, [he] came back, praising God." "He threw himself at Jesus' feet and thanked Him" (Luke 17:16 NIV). In verse 17 of Luke 17, Jesus inquires of the man who returned to thank Him for his being healed, "Were not all ten cleansed? Where are the other nine? Was no one found to return and give praise to God …" Then Jesus told the man, "Rise and go; your faith has made you well" (Luke 17:17 NIV).

This is a glaring illustration into the grace of God! Jesus didn't go to the trouble of demeaning the other nine, as He addressed the one man who returned to thank Jesus. In other words, He only asked about the other nine. He didn't hold the one thankful man responsible, nor did He take him to task for the gracelessness of those nine men who were healed but showed ungrateful behavior. God blesses us with His grace all the time, *whether we thank Him or not!* Ask yourself whether or not you practice showing gratitude toward God for His grace. I've been practicing *gratitude toward God* for some time. I thank Him throughout my day for even the minutest reasons. Doing this keeps me centered and grounded in Jesus through His Holy Spirit. Pragmatically? I can whisper a prayer so that only Jesus and I know I am praying. I do not practice this prayer method to impress anyone. I am communicating with God through the Holy Spirit. In Matthew 6:5–8, Jesus is very clear as to how He expects us to pray. "When you pray, don't be like the hypocrites who pretend piety by praying publicly on street corners ... where everyone can see them. Truly, that is all the reward they will get. When you pray, go away by yourself, all alone, and shut the door behind you and pray secretly, and your Father, who knows your secrets, will reward you" (Matthew 6:5–6 TLB).

Inspired by Psalm 103:1–12, in 1996 I began my "Lord, Thank You ..." log. The first thank-you entry was prompted by my daughter's sincere desire that she have her braces removed in time for her high school senior pictures to be taken. I have maintained this list ever since. Those "important" issues and answers have made it onto the list for more than twenty years. One year, I gave my family a gift, listing all the prayers that God had answered—just for them! It's amazing how many times my family and I have appealed to the Lord for help in our lives. There's a very enjoyable aspect to recording this. From time to time, I will sit and refresh my memory by reading over the list of thank-you's as a reminder of how much the Lord has done for us. Now remember these are just the "important" events that we asked the Lord to intercede in.

I'm reminded of the ten lepers, right? Only one man returned to thank Jesus for His healing. Only one. I try daily to thank Jesus for all that is happening around me. The "Lord, Thank You ..." log was created as a tool to show how grateful I am to the Lord, considering those events having the highest impact in the lives of our family. Since 1996, I have recorded over two hundred thank-you's. Remember these are over two hundred "important" prayers and their answers. Please make being grateful a priority, and start listing those answers to prayers that you are thankful for. You'll see it's amazing!

Reflection: Have you tried to be *deliberate* about being a *gracious* Christ believer? Do you see yourself passing out *gifts of grace* to those you meet, almost like tossing bouquets to grateful receivers?

OUR GREATEST LIFE SOURCE: GOD

The book of Deuteronomy 6:4–12 addresses the subject of acknowledging God as the source of all we have in and out of this world.

> Hear, O Israel: The Lord our God … is one. Love the Lord your God with all your heart and with all your soul and with all your strength … When the Lord your God brings you into the land he swore to your fathers … to give you a land, with large, flourishing cities you did not build, houses filled with all kinds of good things you did not provide … be careful not to forget the Lord, who brought you out of the land of slavery. (Deuteronomy 6:4, 10–12 NIV)

Remembering and acknowledging this is easy to overlook. As a person matures in life, after much hard work, including getting and paying for a quality education and landing their "dream job," it can be easy to forget where, how, and through whom these accomplishments actually originated.

My wife and I have marveled at the impact the Lord has had in the various stages of our life together. We believe none of the great things in our lives could have occurred had it not been for God. Certainly, we have been blessed with some talents, but as we've matured in our physical bodies, we have likewise been measured in the maturing process of our "spiritual bodies." Let me explain. "You shall love the Lord your God with all your heart and with all your soul and with all your strength" (Deuteronomy 6:4 NIV). We have taken this very seriously, acknowledging the Lord's hand in the life we live. Associating the Lord with the activities in our lives *before* they happened and thanking Him for His involvement considering the results because of the Lord's blessings has become a regular occurrence for us. We pray for divine guidance and direction and then express our thanks and praise to God for His answers. It's what we've done for many years.

I've spoken about my having been a worrier. I told you that I feel I got this habit honestly from my mother. Well, one night in trying to consciously be a nonworrier, taking my own advice on how to let the Lord handle the details for me, I practiced what I'd been preaching. We were going to a play that our daughters and granddaughter were in. There were no assigned seats with our tickets, so it was first come, first served. My wife and I went separately, so that she could take her mother to the performance without her having to get to the church early and stand in line for a long time. On the way to the church, I prayed something like "Lord, You know I really [am prone] but hate to worry about things. So Lord, please handle the situation for us." We wanted to get stage-close seats so that my senior citizen mother-in-law would be able to see well. I continued. "Lord, please lead me directly to the seats we should have." With that request, I was being bold with Jesus, because I wanted Him to see that I was all-in with my wanting to be in a nonworrier position. I waited in line, walked into the auditorium, and laid my coat across the seats in plenty of time for my family and a friend to arrive and have perfect seats. We thoroughly enjoyed the show!

The cynic in the crowd would poke great fun at my example. That's OK! The apostle Paul writes in 1 Corinthians 1:18 (NIV) that the Word of the Lord will be "foolishness" to the unbeliever. I get that. I've heard it said that the world says, "Seeing is believing" (a quote from seventeenth-century English clergyman Thomas Fuller). Jesus says, "Blessed are those who have not seen and yet have believed" (John 20:29 NIV). I am perfectly all right with the cynics' disbelief. I can deal with that. Let me tell you that when you walk with the Lord, I mean *closely* with Him, and you open up your life to Him, look out! Your life will be unbelievably *fantastic!*

Along these lines, let me share one more remarkable example of the influence of the Holy Spirit's role in our lives. For some time, the electronic fob needed to unlock my car doors was inoperable. It was used so often that the button on it no longer would open the car door. We discovered that the cost to replace this could range upward of $300 or more! I know.

Why couldn't we just do things the old-fashioned way by inserting the key into the door lock, right? Right! There's only one problem. Not using the fob electronically conveyed to the security system that the car was being broken into! The remedy for that was to set off the very noisy car alarm! So I guess you can see that replacing the fob was really a terrific idea.

We shopped around. One day, needing to replace an out-of-the-ordinary battery for a calculator at home, as we shopped in a battery specialty store, we asked about the possibility and the cost of replacing the fob for the car. Yes, they could replace the fob. They had a generic blank fob model in stock that would accommodate my vehicle. And what's more, it was about $150 less expensive. God provided once again!

I get it! But the everyday nonbeliever *won't* get it. My wife and I have begun recognizing the course of the happenings within our lives that just *have to be* the leading of the Holy Spirit. We just can't make this stuff up!

The prophet Samuel was directed by the Lord, "Fill your horn with oil and be on your way [to the home of Jesse of Bethlehem]. I have chosen one of his sons to be king" (1 Samuel 16:1 NIV). Admittedly, Samuel was afraid of the reaction that King Saul would have, finding out that in obedience to God, Samuel had anointed another man as the future king of Israel. Here is the point of my bringing up this story of Samuel. As Samuel pondered the logistics of his task, the Lord said to him, "I will *show* you what to do" (italics added; 1 Samuel 16:3 NIV). As the Lord promised to *show* Samuel what to do, I believe the Lord will *show* everyone what to do in their lives, if they will believe it's so. I cannot stress enough the incredible power involved with the leading of the Holy Spirit. And be reminded that I fully expect there to be those who will think this is just groundless! Remember? The Word of the Lord will be "foolishness" to those who do not believe (1 Corinthians 1:18 NIV). I get it!

Reflection: What might you be experiencing that you may pray for the same direction from the Lord that Samuel received? "I will *show* you what to do" (1 Samuel 16:3 NIV).

SERIOUS, PRACTICAL LIFE-WALKING WITH THE HOLY SPIRIT: I WOULDN'T HAVE IT ANY OTHER WAY

In the book of John, we read, "It is best for you that I go away, because if I don't, the Advocate [Comforter, Encourager, or Counselor] won't come. If I go away, then I will send him to you" (John 16:7 NLT). How wonderful it is to know that I have an advocate, a comforter, an encourager, a counselor, who will walk with me *daily—every second*—if only I will believe, acknowledge, and let Him into my life! As it is written, God promises, "I will never, *never* fail you nor forsake you" (Hebrews 13:5 TLB).

I've heard it preached that God knew about all of us as early as His creation of the world. Imagine a God who is *that powerful and magnificent!* God knows *you* and me, and He has empowered the Holy Spirit to be our advocate, comforter, encourager, and counselor to aid us through our lives. I can tell you that I talk with my comforter when I get discouraged. He then encourages me. When I don't know what to do or where to turn, my counselor guides me. I cannot begin to suppose or imagine a life without the Holy Spirit. I *don't want* to imagine such a life!

One of the reasons I decided to write this book has to do with how important I know living with the Holy Spirit is in my life. I start a typical day by preparing physically and hygienically, thus keeping my place in society. When I was working, my spiritual day started by using the *Our Daily Bread* devotional as a guide to Bible reading for that day.

For some time now, I have taken my faith walk to a different level. The knowledge of the presence of the Holy Spirit walking with me in life has become so very real. The basis of my belief stems from Jesus Christ Himself. Jesus said, "If you love me, keep my commands. And I will ask the Father, and he will give you another advocate to help you and be with you forever—the Spirit of truth" (John 14:15–17 NKJV). Taken earnestly, walking with the Holy Spirit will totally and wonderfully change your life.

You need not ever feel alone. The advocate, the Holy Spirit, is always near. The Holy Spirit wants to be in on everything you do, think, say—every aspect of your life! When you turn your life over to and believe in Jesus, acknowledging His presence, accepting His free gift of salvation, and doing all that you can to positively change your lifestyle, the Holy Spirit will live with your spirit. Do that, and then watch out! Your life will never be the same!

The Holy Spirit walks with you throughout your day. My wife, Lee Ann, and I appreciate the timing of the Holy Spirit. When you literally turn your life and the activities of it over to God, the Holy Spirit can handle the details of your everyday life. I am reminded of a time when I had a few errands to run and an impromptu meeting ensued. Lee Ann had the plumbers coming to check the furnaces of our daughter Ellen's house and ours, so I wasn't too worried about the time I had to do all that I had on my plate. Lee Ann accompanied the plumber to Ellen's house first. It *just so happened* that our daughter Jamie *needed something from our house* (not too critical, but necessary). Had the plumbers worked at our house first, Lee Ann would not have been home when Jamie later came by. You see, we believe the Holy Spirit directed Lee Ann to schedule the day's activities according to the practical needs of our family. Believe it or not, we live this way, and we thank the Lord for His closeness and watching out for our every need. I know there are skeptics out there. Don't knock it until you've tried it!

Another instance has to do with my political involvement, after having been off the board of commissioners for one term. Having tied another candidate in an election, he was appointed to the board, and I was not. Four years later, I ran for election and won the race overwhelmingly. In that campaign, I had run on a no-tax-increase platform. The board was in the throes of arriving at a budget for the following year. At least three of the members were satisfied with raising the tax rate to fund the township expenditures for the upcoming year. Doing that would leave what I considered an excessive balance in the township's reserves. In a budget hearing, I pushed for not raising the taxes to no immediate advantage for the township residents. At the next meeting, the issue was once again discussed. I asked the board president to review the balance sheet again, eliminating the increase. It turned out that there still was a substantive reserve anyway. After a healthy discussion, at least two of the other members joined me in not implementing the tax increase. When I got home later that evening, I said to my wife, "Honey, give me a *great big kiss!*" She complied but asked me why, and I told her, "It's because I convinced the board to hold the line on taxes for next year." She replied, "I was praying for you [to have that happen]!" That's "serious, practical *life-walking*" in action. I believe that God wants to be a part of our lives, wherever our lives take us. *No*. I should have said, "I believe that God wants to be a part of our lives, wherever *God* takes our lives."

Throughout the day, I am often just thanking God for even the little, everyday happenings in my life. I'll just whisper, "Thank You, Lord," and keep on going. Without sounding corny or being sacrilegious at all, I feel like the Holy Spirit might be considered a *Who Wants to Be a Millionaire?* lifeline." Or maybe we could look at Him as if he is a "Cash Cab mobile shout-out." Nevertheless, know that if you allow it, the Holy Spirit will be *ever present* for you in every aspect of your life. Praise God!

When you surrender your life to Christ, He will go with you throughout your day and then some, every day. Having said that, I should warn you that there will be those who won't like or appreciate *the new you*. Jesus spoke about that too. He said, "The world cannot accept him [the Holy Spirit], because it neither sees him nor knows him. But you know him, for he lives with you and will be in you" (John 14:17 NIV). Admittedly, this takes faith.

I see faith as something that needs to be developed *and exercised* to grow stronger. In some ways, it works as a trial-and-error situation. I'm sure you've heard it said that Missouri is "the Show-Me State," where allegedly the people who live there are the ultimate skeptics, right? They have to be shown stuff before they'll believe it. In 2 Corinthians 5:6–8, we hear Paul counseling us as to how we should live. In verse 7, chapter 5 (NIV), we read, "We live by faith, not by sight." It could be said, "The world says, 'Seeing is believing'; God says, 'Believing is seeing.'" The mystery of it is that praying and waiting for answers can have troubling results at times. Our prayers are sometimes answered in ways that we either hadn't asked for and/or are not to our liking. We at times may be troubled by the answers. These situations challenge our faith, but belief in the One True God ultimately gets the reward: heaven forever!

So "serious, practical life-walking" involves faith. Hebrews 11:1 (NIV) reads, "Now faith is being sure of what we hope for and certain of what we do not see." I have come to a place in my life where I possibly accept all of living on faith. "Faith in what?" you ask. I serve a risen Savior—Jesus—and a Good God. I know that He loves me! Because He loves me, He wouldn't do anything to intentionally hurt me. "Serious, practical life-walking" means that I will continue to take chances. I will risk living my life with God, because He has never let me down—*ever!*

Reflection: Have you prayed about *getting serious* regarding your involvement with a sincere, personal "walk" with God, where you put your life in His hands and trust that He will help you, never letting you down?

MIRACLES STILL HAPPEN: PROOF FROM PERSONAL EXPERIENCE

The world defines a miracle as "a highly improbable or extraordinary event, development, or accomplishment that brings very welcome consequences" (Google.com/searchmiracle). In the *Illustrated Davis Dictionary of the Bible*, a miracle is defined as "wonders, signs, types, powers, works of God." I am drawn to this topic because of a conversation I once had with a friend.

My friend was a fairly new Christian. It took him quite a while before he was able to surrender his life to the control of our Lord Jesus Christ. He was one of the most honest men I had ever known, and before he committed to anything, he did a thorough due diligence of his own choosing and purpose. In the case of his consideration of becoming a Christian, he wrestled with a number of issues. One that was hampering him was his own life's history. Growing up as a child, there wasn't a lot of love in the home. His parents were not supportive of the children, and out of his siblings, his youngest brother was the person he loved the best. Ironically, his brother was the child most picked on by their father.

In reality, if it weren't for the Lord in our lives, my friend and I would have very little in common. To contrast our home lives, my own brother and I could not have been more blessed by God. Our parents were absolutely amazing! They supported and loved us in so many ways growing up. An example of this was when my brother and I decided to go over the road in a part-time gospel singing ministry. Our parents bought us a brand-new, full-sized van to haul our sound equipment and instruments. How many middle-class parents with a mortgage and car payments would do *that*?

When my friend's younger brother was diagnosed as being in the final stages of cancer, he and his wife prepared a written packet of scripture for the brother to read. My friend's deepest personal feelings about his recently found faith were included for the brother's consideration. The brother initially called my friend to tell him that there "had never been any religion in [his] life before" and he didn't want any now. Eventually, the brother's opinion changed, and we rejoiced that he had accepted the Lord's free gift of salvation and he gained eternal life with Christ.

One day my friend stopped by to pay us a visit. Knowing about his dying brother, I could tell from his body language that he hadn't just stopped in for a friendly, social call. I was right. We talked about how this friend should react to his brother's death. He shared that he was probably going to be "pretty mad" at God. I confessed that I didn't have any pat answers for him, because other than losing my parents and grandmothers, I had not yet had to mourn the loss of my brother or any siblings-in-law. In a sermon sometime in my lifetime, the speaker said that Jesus came to earth as a human being so that He would experience all the feelings, even temptations that we humans face every day. My friend said, "I hear people talk about miracles." He inferred as much as to say, "Where is God here and now when my brother needs a miracle?" So we talked about the topic of miracles. I decided to share two stories of miraculous events I have experienced.

The first story involves an African American student named Tyrel (not his real name). Tyrel behaved as if he was not interested in learning in my classroom. He would continually be talking and fooling around with other students, preventing them from paying attention and of course limiting his own learning. This type of behavior went against the grain in my classroom. I was an "old school" type of teacher—teachers taught students who behaved themselves and learned. Needless to say, after maybe a week of these conditions, I made a phone call home. Tyrel came from a racially mixed, single-parent household. Tyrel's mother was Caucasian, and his father was African American, which will prove to be significant later in the story.

When I called the home, I had a very frank and open conversation about Tyrel and his behavior in my classroom. Tyrel's mother was very supportive, and she understood the importance of the type of behavior I needed and expected in my classroom. His mom told me that I was "not the only teacher to have contacted [her]" informing her of Tyrel's poor behavior. She told me that she would have a discussion with her son and that I should look for his actions to be more of what I needed and expected. I ended the phone conversation feeling as if good progress was possible and I could expect Tyrel to behave much better going forward. Actually, Tyrel was relatively speaking a positively different young man the days after his mother and I spoke.

Soon after, the time for parent-teacher conferences was upon us. Our teacher team wanted to meet with Tyrel's parents regarding his behavior. When it came time for the conference, before I spoke, I waited until after my colleagues had shared their experiences concerning Tyrel. Expecting to get the support I had previously received from the mother, I began to share that although Tyrel had been showing improvement, his behavior was still not where I needed it to be. Well, here's where the situation got interesting. The mom launched into a tirade at me about how Tyrel had been sharing that "all the other kids are acting just like [Tyrel was acting], and he is being picked on because he is Black …" Since I had never previously been accused of such an allegation, I really didn't know what to say. I believe my colleagues were equally astounded, and no one uttered a word. I just ended my report, and the conference concluded. Tyrel was present for the entire parent-teacher conference, so he witnessed his mother's accusations toward me.

During the next few weeks, it was almost impossible for me to teach. Tyrel took every opportunity to disrupt my teaching. He would get up in the middle of the lesson and prance around the room as he went "to get a tissue," taking the occasion to mess with his friends and just be obviously distracting for all of us.

I have told people that I did not go to school without first praying about my upcoming day. One morning I prayed, "Lord, what would *possess* Tyrel to act the way he's been acting [in my classroom]?" Almost immediately, the thought occurred to me, *Maybe he* is *possessed!* At that moment, my prayer went something like this: "In the mighty name of Jesus Christ, through the power of the Holy Spirit, demon, *be cast out* of Tyrel!" I share with you that I had never before considered being a part of something like this. In fact, my family was friends with a couple where the woman had gotten into dealing with demons, casting them out of people, etc., and it ruined her marriage. Her husband wasn't comfortable and wished she would stop doing it. Nevertheless, I went to school believing that if a demon had been possessing Tyrel, the demon had been cast out of him.

At school when it was time for the students to arrive, I took the post for my morning duty in the hall by my classroom. I waited for my homeroom students to arrive. As I stood there, I looked to my left and saw Tyrel coming my way. My thought was *Oh man, here he comes* … only to have Tyrel walk up to and stop right in front of me, get right in my face, and say, "Mr. Schin, I'm sorry for the way I've been acting in your class, and it will never happen again." Wow! I can still recall how stunned and blown away I felt, yet somehow, I immediately realized an amazingly wonderful blessing as well. I thanked Tyrel, and he went on his way. I remember raising my hand to God to acknowledge my thanks and to praise Him, right there in the hall! I imagine anyone around me must have thought I was losing it or something. I must confess that I do not recall sharing the story with anyone, missing a tremendous witnessing opportunity. I should have been bolder for the Lord.

Tyrel behaved as I'd hoped he would for the rest of the school year. A few years later, at a street fair, my family and I met Tyrel and his mother and siblings, and there were very cordial and kind things said on all accounts. It was obvious that Tyrel was no longer tormented or possessed. What *a miracle!*

My friend's response to this story was "If someone wasn't a believer before, after hearing that story, they certainly would become one." Well said, don't you think?

The next miracle story involves a mission trip I was taking to Seaford, Delaware, on a very rainy Friday afternoon and night. Due to a late departure from a school obligation, my trip was seemingly off to a bad start. Not having had the luxury of GPS at the time, I had painstakingly mapped out a course of travel from Pennsylvania to Seaford. My plan was to go south into Maryland. Shortly after crossing the PA/MD line I would follow a northern route a short distance to a direct route into Seaford. This was supposed to be a direct, easy-to-follow course of travel. I expected to arrive at the church in Seaford just in time for dinner and the Friday evening program—at about six o'clock.

We all know or have at least heard about Murphy's law. Well, my father explained that *our family* was plagued by something he called "Schin luck." Sure enough, it was possible that something could go wrong, and it did!

You may recall my saying that "Shortly after crossing the PA/MD line I would follow a northern route a short distance to a direct route into Seaford." So by now the weather had turned ugly and I was traveling in a driving rainstorm! After crossing the PA/MD line, I forgot to take the northern route; I continued to drive south into Maryland. This would later prove to be a major mistake. As I was charting my course at home earlier in the week, I was careful to plan not to navigate the I-95/I-695 corridor interstate system in southern Maryland. These routes can be very confusing unless a person travels them regularly, which I had not.

After traveling for quite some time, I felt uneasy as I began reading signs for Baltimore and other Maryland destinations with no mention of Delaware anywhere! Then I found myself confronted with what I had preferred to avoid: the I-95/I-695 corridor interstate system in southern Maryland.

I pulled off the road onto the shoulder and turned off the car. Feeling totally helpless, I began to pray. At this point, it was after six o'clock, I had already missed an important 5:30 team meeting, and everyone at the church was enjoying a meal and fellowship before the evening's activities. I called the church and someone in the office answered. I explained my situation, asking the person to tell the weekend coordinator that I was lost but on my way, and I asked them to keep me in their prayers. He said he would pass along my message.

OK, I thought, as cars and trucks whizzed past me along the highway, *Lord, what should I do now?* I started the car and drove until there was an exit where I could get off the highway. Understand the blinding rain had continued throughout the night, now coming in horizontal sheets. Having exited the highway, I came upon a convenience store/gas station. My dad was a huge believer in asking mail carriers and gasoline station attendants for directions if lost.

Now thanks for having read my story to this point. If you've stayed with me this far, *don't leave and miss this miracle!*

So I shut off the car and grabbed a pencil, a notepad, and the map I always carried with me. I walked into the store. It was slightly busy at the time. The man behind the counter was waiting on patrons, so I didn't immediately look to him for help. As I moved about the store, a woman, having noticed me, asked, "Are you looking for directions?" Now knowing me, I wanted to say, "Duh! No, I always walk around on rainy nights with a map, a pencil, and a notepad …" But being desperately in need and having prayed for help, I said yes. I told the woman that I was trying to get to Seaford.

Don't miss the *miracle!*

This dear woman said, "Wait right here." She went out to a car that was being fueled and left me standing in the store. When she returned, she said, "I'm a bus driver; I was just in Seaford yesterday." She handed me a paper and said, "Here are your directions to Seaford."

I told you not to miss *the miracle!*

Needless to say, I was late to the mission. I missed the entire first night's program, but the next day, when I gathered with the rest of the team, I had an incredible experience to witness about! And I have been witnessing to this miracle ever since. I'm sure it has to be at least fifteen years ago that this happened.

My friend was once again astonished by this story. Amazed, he remarked, "Again, if you weren't a believer before, you sure *would be* after hearing that story."

Miracles do happen! From my experiences, miracles happen every day. People are prayed for, saved from near-death encounters, and yes, good, well-wishing individuals are there when they are needed to lend a hand— to give a lost and confused driver direction on a rainy night. It has been my belief that Christ left the Holy Spirit with the disciples to be their constant companion, through whose power Christ's work could be accomplished.

I am living proof that God wants to be with us in every aspect of our lives! There is nothing too big or too small for Him to handle. Be careful not to make the mistake of asking Jesus and the Holy Spirit into only those areas of your life that you think you cannot accomplish on your own.

Some scripture to take seriously in this regard can be read in Proverbs 16:3, 7, and 9 (NIV). In Proverbs 16:3 (NIV), we are encouraged, "Commit to the Lord whatever you do, and your plans will succeed." Proverbs 16:7 (NIV) states, "When a man's ways are pleasing to the Lord, he makes even his enemies live at peace with him." Proverbs 16:9 (NIV) tells us, "In his heart a man plans his course, but the Lord determines his steps."

The verses in Proverbs 16 remarkably match the miracles that I've shared above. When I was selected to be a member of the mission team that weekend, I had "committed to the Lord" what I would be doing in His name. The weekend's purpose and the event itself qualified as being "pleasing to the Lord." God certainly needed to determine my steps that rainy night, somewhere in Maryland. The only viable option that I saw would have ended poorly, because I would have turned around and gone home. Whatever role I had in the effort that weekend would have been abandoned. God's mission would not have been the complete success story He'd planned.

So you can see, where God's ministry is concerned, the promises that He makes are *real*. As believers we need to be mindful of the impact God's Word can have on our lives! Christ, through the Holy Spirit, wants to be with us each day and in every aspect of our daily living. If we are walking with Christ, we should be able and willing to *include* Christ in all that we say and do.

Reflection: Is there something that you can take to the Lord in prayer and have it be part of *a miracle?*

GIVING IS THE CHRISTIAN THING TO DO

> For if you give, you will get! Your gift will return to you in full and overflowing measure, pressed down, shaken together to make room for more, and running over. Whatever measure you use to give—large or small—will be used to measure what is given back to you. (Luke 6:38 TLB)

My wife and I met at church. Our families were active in the life of the church. I am sure we often heard sermons about something called *tithing*, which is a tenth of an individual's income being pledged to the church. The church where we met used different methods to reach out to the members to garner pledges for giving, which they used to help them put together an annual budget. As entry-level bank employees, and being newlyweds, we were able to pay our bills, but there wasn't much left over for something called "discretionary spending."

I don't know if either of us knew whether our parents tithed. We cannot be sure that we had any personal role models when it came to giving. But we certainly started our lives together as tithers.

We were married for about a year when it came to our attention that although we *were* tithing, my wife pointed out that we "weren't tithing correctly." I recall asking the logical question "What do you mean by tithing 'correctly'?" She said, "We're tithing on our take-home pay; we should be tithing on the gross amount" (the amount that we were actually earning).

Now I gotta tell ya that discovery of my wife's seemed like one, it was her being *really picky,* and two, I thought, *Man! We barely have enough money to live on now, and you want to give away more?* Well, I have a news flash for all who will listen. "You can't *outgive* God!" After we decided to start giving God 10 percent of what we *actually made*—you know before taxes are deducted—my wife and I went from barely making it to more easily paying our bills, with a little bit more left over.

So I'm sure this all sounds moderately interesting, but why am I bringing it up here? LeeAnn, my lovely wife and best friend for more than forty-five years, has not worked full-time outside the household since before our children were born, with the exception of a partial year after she finished college late in life, when the kids were in their teenage years.

As time went by, we were able to put a little money away, but we weren't saving money the way one would expect we should have been saving. Honestly, I rarely made a living that anyone would ever envy. In fact, there were several times when I was out of work and had to get a new job. Early in my career, pension plans required a worker to be participating in a plan for at least ten years to become vested—to be able to collect a benefit upon retirement. In those days, I was interested in moving up the ladder, and sometimes I found a new company and their "ladder" to do so. The longest I ever worked anywhere was when I taught school. I taught for eighteen years, and it was the most rewarding work I have ever done! I like to say, "It's the hardest thing I've ever done and not considered it a 'job.'"

Keep in mind we have tithed for all the years, through all the job changes and stints out of work, and we are now retired. My worst fear was that I would retire but still need to get at least a part-time job. I remember that when my dad retired at sixty-five years old (on his birthday, I'll have you know), there were coworkers who got full-time jobs and went right back to work. Dad said, "If I'd wanted to work, I wouldn't have retired!" That's kind of how I looked at it also.

I met with a retirement counselor, and we laid out the path that I would follow. Without going into any details, let me just say that I won't need to get a part-time job now, unless I want to spare my wife and be out of the house more for her sake and sanity.

We have just been blessed so much by God. My wife and I tithed throughout our life together. I recall many years ago an incident that I don't think went unnoticed by God. I'd received a $10,000 profit-sharing bonus while working at a financial institution. Being a true tither, we gave a $1,000 donation to the church, right before losing that employment. Hearing that I was temporarily out of work, the pastor asked me if I wanted my money back. Not just a little surprised, but thankful for his thinking of us, I answered in the negative. My wife and I believed that we would be employed once again and shortly.

It appears to us that God has been looking out for us all these years. There was very little intentional preparation for retirement. It hasn't necessarily been mismanagement on our parts; we just have not had a lot of money to be able to save. But we have given willingly and joyfully to the work of God all these years. Even when there wasn't money coming in, the Lord made a way for us to continue on. Interestingly enough, we even tithed from my unemployment compensation.

This is not a book about practical money management. We simply want to stress that God has rewarded us for our diligently giving Him back some of the money that we believe is all His in the first place. I have heard the expression "I'd tithe if I only made more money!" What a foolish thing to say. Tithing is not about *the money*; *it's about faith*. Have faith that God will provide, and He will see you through.

My wife and I are living Luke 6:38 (TLB). "For if you give, you will get! Your gift will return to you in full and overflowing measure, pressed down, shaken together to make room for more, and running over. Whatever measure you used to give—large or small—will be used to measure what is given back to you." We gave, and now in retirement, God is being faithful. And we are so very grateful.

Reflection: Have you come to the point where you realize that giving to God is *not about* the *money?* Can you see instead that *it's about* how much *faith* you have *in God's power* to "handle life" for you? Will you trust the Lord to provide for you?

THOSE THAT WAIT UPON THE LORD

Isaiah 40:27–31

The members of my family have been generally blessed with good health. Steady employment has typically also been in our favor. Commitment to spouses has been the model, so legal issues have not been an issue in this regard. Unhealthy sibling rivalries have not occurred either, excusing the early childhood squabbles that all families encounter. The truth of the matter is that our family has gathered at Thanksgiving Day celebrations for many years, thanks to our brothers- and sisters-in-law in Pennsylvania and New Jersey.

So you might ask, "How can you even begin to talk about 'troubles' discussed in Isaiah 40:27? You've never had to face 'troubles' as you have described your life and the lives of your family members."

Well, I stated that the members of my family have been *generally blessed* with good health. Without going into any gory details, our extended family members have undergone surgeries, deaths, and other circumstances. Actually, my parents each had had surgeries, and I experienced triple-bypass, open-heart surgery when I was only fifty-seven years old. You know, it's amazing how parents can be such important role models for their children of *all* ages.

When my mother was in her early seventies, she underwent some type of non-life-threatening surgery. By the way, do you know how you can tell whether or not a surgical procedure is "major"? If it's *happening to you*, consider it "major." Before having her surgery, she commented something along the line of "I'm not afraid. The Lord will take care of this." Now my mom stood just about five feet tall, and she was the softest-spoken, most loving woman. She thrived on being behind the scenes, unlike my entertainer-type dad. They complemented each other oh so very well.

As I prepared myself for *my* heart surgery, I took my mother's example into consideration. I thought, *If this dear little woman can trust God in this way, why shouldn't I?* I tried to reassure my family, and I prayed the Lord's will over my life. I requested that my pastor pray over me before going into surgery, and I was determined to go into the procedure as calmly as I could. I had this idea that my body would respond better during and after the surgery if I wasn't tense and upset. (You know, I really didn't discuss this medically with my surgeon, but I thought it couldn't hurt to try it anyway.) My brother-in-law called to wish me well the night before my surgery, and then during a post surgery conversation, he remarked something like "You were pretty cool when I talked with you over the phone the night before the operation." I told him that I used my mother as my model and that I was leaving the entire situation up to God.

So waiting upon the Lord in a world where we all expect instantaneous answers or results has become almost passé for most of society. Isaiah writes,

> No one can fathom the depths of his understanding. He gives power to the tired and worn out, and strength to the weak. But they that wait upon the Lord shall renew their strength. They shall mount up with wings like eagles; they shall run and not be weary; they shall walk and not faint.
> (Isaiah 40:28–29, 31 TLB)

Think with me for a moment about a time when you were presented with a decision you had to make and it seemed that the answer regarding the decision was needed *right now!* What did you do? Did you consider all the options? Did you talk with a trusted friend, relative, or former teachers you know? If the answer is in the affirmative, good for you! Going a little bit out on a limb, I am going to assume the outcome was a success or a win.

There was a time when, in order to save some money by quitting our membership at the fitness gym, we purchased a piece of exercise equipment. It was an elliptical machine—a nice one! The unit cost was in excess of $1,200. I felt I had done my homework, and I thought my wife was on board with the purchase. The unit arrived in a large box, and as usual, my wife put it together. I followed my typical pattern. I strategically held the flashlight and read the directions as my wife wielded the wrenches and screwdrivers. Hey! Don't mock. Have you ever tried to construct something in the dark? Strategic flashlight holding is a necessary art!

So the machine was built and ready for use! My wife said, "Well, you ordered it. You should be the first one to use it." I eagerly climbed onto it and tried it out. As it turned out, even with it set on the lowest level of difficulty, neither my wife nor I could use this enough for it to be of any help to us. In retrospect, when we looked at the TV commercials showing this, those demonstrating it were not senior citizens but young people.

I hadn't talked with a trusted friend, relative, or former teacher, even though I'd been working with many. The fact that I had viewed the commercials and looked on the internet did nothing to ensure my successful purchase, and we were not able to use the machine. I did not quit the gym.

Remember what Isaiah writes? "No one can fathom the depths of his understanding" (Isaiah 40:28 TLB). God understands us and notices us and the circumstances we encounter. He wants to be involved in the "everyday stuff" that we have to face in life. All we need to do is to *let Him in!* We did not *let Him in.* We went on the internet, we watched the TV commercials, but that's all! Looking into the rearview mirror on this situation, we did not make a wise, educated, well-informed decision.

"He gives power to the tired and worn out, and strength to the weak" (Isaiah 40:29 TLB). This decision became a problem for my wife and me—actually more for *me* because, you see, my wife (as it turned out) had not really done any of her own due diligence regarding this purchase. So every day, every week, every month that this exercise machine just stood in the basement, not being used, the wrong decision continued to be a reminder. It's safe to say that I was the tired and worn out one in our family.

"But they that wait upon the Lord shall renew their strength. They shall mount up with wings like eagles; they shall run and not be weary; they shall walk and not faint" (Isaiah 40:31 TLB). I finally began to pray about what we could do to get out from under this dilemma. Yes, I prayed about it!

Now for those skeptics out there, I admit that I did more than just pray. Did you know that the expression "The Lord helps those who help themselves" is *not* found anywhere in the Bible? Nope. That's just a phrase that has been developed somewhere by someone along the way.

But truth be known, I *did* try to help myself. I started speaking to people about the machine, I tried to *give it away*, but oddly no one wanted or needed an elliptical machine. So there it stood, as a brutal reminder of my mistake.

One day, I mentioned to my assistant principal that I had this equipment. Since he was a professional bodybuilder, I thought he would be a good resource while in my pickle. He came by the house and saw it. He thought he might be able to find a buyer for us. He found someone who, having seen the pictures of the machine, decided to buy it. I am still grateful for the help.

By finally asking for help with my predicament, I was "waiting upon the Lord."

"The Lord renewed [my] strength … [I] mounted up with wings like [an] eagle; [I] did run and [was] not weary; [I] walked and [did] not faint" (Isaiah 40:31 TLB). The Lord taught me quite a lesson. I lost about $700 on the elliptical machine, but I was reminded that I need to go to the Lord with decisions because "no one can fathom the depth of [God's] understanding" (Isaiah 40:28 TLB). God will intervene in our daily activities, but He won't meddle in our business. We ask; He answers.

Reflection: Think back to a critical decision you've made over your lifetime, and imagine the potential outcome had you employed the steps outlined in this section. What might have been the result had you *asked for help* and *waited upon the Lord*?

THE PATH TO A LONG AND SATISFYING LIFE

Proverbs 3:1–6

King Solomon wrote in Proverbs 3, "If you want a long and satisfying life, closely follow my instructions" (Proverbs 3:1 TLB). I might add, "If you want a long and satisfying life, never forget to be truthful and kind" (Proverbs 3:2 TLB).

God's Word, and my dad's here, is terrific counsel. My father used to say, "If you never tell a lie, you'll never get caught in one." Just another one of the wise sayings and practices of my dad. As he began to adhere to this belief, I am fairly certain that he didn't know that he was quoting Old Testament scripture. I believe my folks practiced this because other than untruthfully telling me that there was a Santa Claus when I was a little kid, I know of no other instance where they mislead me. *Wait!* You mean there *isn't a Santa Claus?* "Yes, Virginia, there is a Santa Claus …" is what I've read every year at Christmas time on the editorial page of the local newspaper.

A funny story about my dad and his advice about always being truthful. There was a radio station running a call-in contest called "Father Mows Best" leading up to the Father's Day holiday. If you were the fifth caller to the station, the DJ would take your call and ask you to give some sage truth statement for sharing with the listening audience. My call went through, and I shared Dad's advice "If you never tell a lie, you'll never get caught in one." Well, wouldn't you know? My name was drawn, and I won a Penn State riding mower! It was delivered to the house, and the delivery was broadcasted *live* over the radio! I got a number of friends who heard it and called to tell me so. One neighbor was late to work because he just *had to drive* to the house and share in my good fortune.

"If you want a long and satisfying life … never forget to be truthful and kind. Hold these virtues tightly. Write them deep within your heart" (Proverbs 3:3 TLB). As if being truthful isn't hard enough, now God piles on by telling us to be *kind* as well! Come on, God! *Really?* Have you ever assessed the "difficulty ratio" involving the number of people who cross your path, with the challenges that they present to you, the behavior with which they conduct themselves (not *kind* or *considerate*), and then looking at them and needing to force yourself to be *kind?* I'm not sure how to measure this, but I truly believe the odds of being consistently kind, depending on using my own behavioral resources, are not very favorable.

Considering this scenario just from the standpoint of selfish motives, using the perspective of cause and effect, it might slant this way: "If—wanting a satisfying life, then—being kind." Well, that is one way the everyday person might look at this. So you say, "Well, that's a start, isn't it?" Yes, yes, that's a start. Do you think that God spoke to King Solomon with that slant in mind?

I personally do not think that God necessarily was using a quid pro quo in this counseling offered to Solomon. Kindness cannot be accomplished without help. For me, the Holy Spirit's help is a *must*. Without God's assistance, I would be unable to pull off the kindness element for this equation:

Truth + Kindness = a Satisfying Life

Throughout my personal and business life, the people I've come in contact with have basically been honest. Unfortunately, I can't say the same for the behavior I have endured from some of the political competitors I've faced. Sometimes people twist the truth and tell outright falsehoods, just to win elections. In those cases, even though I might have lost an election because I wouldn't stoop to those low levels, I didn't jeopardize my *satisfying life*. Enough said about that.

Proverbs 3:4 and 5 (TLB) provide us with a directive that if followed can only serve to improve your life. King Solomon writes, "If you want favor with both God and man, and a reputation for good judgment and common sense, then trust the Lord completely; don't ever trust yourself ... Favor with both God and man ..." Who wouldn't wish for these? To be able to get along with our fellow man is half the battle in life. *Loving ourselves* is the other half. There may be an argument for stating that if we don't love ourselves, it'll be *almost impossible* to love others. We have all come in contact with unlovable people. These are the types of folks who roll out on the wrong side of the bed, which is what my father used to say if he thought I was in some type of a bad mood. He'd say, "What's the matter with you? Did you get up on the wrong side of the bed this morning?" That was my cue to pull it together and lose the funk.

According to King Solomon, the remedy for unpleasantness is *complete trust in the Lord*. So I chose *favor with man* to talk about first. God is not really second in my mind. Trust, complete trust in the Lord, will bring favor with God. But it doesn't end there!

A reputation for good judgment and common sense are also the reward for complete trust in the Lord. *Such a deal!* The old saying "Which came first, the chicken or the egg?" might come into play here. Another "Bill Schinism" was "It takes an entire lifetime to develop a good reputation, but you can lose it all in just an instant" of poor decision-making. We are able to see this at many levels in the public as well as the private sectors of society.

What type of reputation have you developed? How do people see you? Are you consistent in your behavior? I once worked for a man—he was a multimillionaire—who used to say, "I hate to be anticipated." I get that. I'm not talking about that. I am asking you whether or not the people you interact with view you highly. Do they see you as someone they can't trust? And what about *common sense?*

The term *common sense* has always set my teeth on edge, and here's why. So you're working with someone older, for me either my father or father-in-law. Admitting I have no affinity for construction or very much about mechanical stuff. I either do or not do something that other more experienced people would know about. They say, "That's just common sense!" For me, it seems like you have to have a certain degree or basic knowledge in an area in order to be able to claim *common sense* in a given situation.

Therefore, it is logical to trust the Lord completely. *Good judgment* is an additional reward for total trust in the Lord. Wow! Trusting in the Lord *completely* seems like a winner type of lifestyle for so many reasons, doesn't it?

The last thing to be said here is "In everything you do, put God first, and He will direct you and crown your efforts with success" (Proverbs 3:6 TLB). Do you want to be successful, the type of successes awarded by and in God's favor? Then sell out to God. Stay close to His Holy Spirit. Be intentional and include the Lord in your daily activities. Start your days with Him—Bible reading and prayer—and finish your days the same way.

As a young Christian, I asked my older cousin, who was a Christian, "Victor, what if all this Christianity stuff is just a hoax?" His answer has stuck with me for more than fifty years! He said, "Even if it *is* all a hoax, you will never find a better lifestyle to live by than what Jesus has taught us." That's a great answer, and *I know* that kind of life. You can have this life too. Just *ask Jesus to come into your heart, and He will!*

Reflection: Have you become discouraged by the behavior of those around you, those with whom you work or play? Do you potentially envy them making you question just who's and what's right anymore? Why not put the kindness equation into effect for yourself?

Truth + Kindness = a Satisfying Life

THE TRUTH ABOUT HOW TO LIVE THE CHRISTIAN LIFE

Galatians 5:16, 18–26 (TLB)

The apostle Paul wrote to the Christians at Galatia in the year AD 49. Interestingly enough, that was about 1,900 years before I was born (just a bit of useless trivia). There were Jewish leaders who were telling new Christians that to be saved, they had to continue to obey the traditional Jewish laws— the most important and sacrificial ritual being the circumcision of the men. Paul, being well-educated in the Jewish religion, spent years condemning Christians to death. After his Damascus Road conversion experience, when he was blinded by a light and saw and heard Jesus speak, he wrote to the Christians in Galatia about the truth of the gospel. The old law was replaced when Christ came to earth by God's direction and plan and was crucified, died, and buried. But the story didn't end there! Jesus rose from the dead and ascended to heaven, so that all those who believe and live in Him will receive an eternal home with God. Thank You, Jesus!

"I advise you to obey only the Holy Spirit's instructions. He will tell you where to go and what to do, and then you won't always be doing the wrong things your evil nature wants you to" (Galatians 5:16 TLB). *Obey only the Holy Spirit's instructions.* And how by chance are we supposed to accomplish *that*?

We've previously discussed walking with the Holy Spirit. Through prayer, scripture reading, other meditation, interaction with fellow Christians, the reading of Christian authors, and intentionally dwelling on the things of God, we can receive "instructions" from the Holy Spirit.

You may recall in the section regarding miracles I knew I had received a word from the Holy Spirit about what to do about the uncooperative, demon-possessed student in my classroom. I *heard* from the Holy Spirit that morning at home during my devotional time.

Admittedly, as I've previously explained, spiritual growth in Christ needs to be established for this to happen. To live for Christ takes discipline. Maybe that's where the term disciple came from. You can't be in a hurry all the time. Listening to or for a word from the Holy Spirit demands we put ourselves in the position, location, and proper atmosphere for this to happen.

I don't know about you, but I don't like the side of me that Paul was describing here. The wrong things of my evil nature are not the traits I wish to disclose to the world! Putting my best foot forward was the way I was brought up. I have always and still *do* want to make my parents proud and not to embarrass my family because there are people still alive who remember Bill and Marie Schin. Having been raised by members of "the Greatest Generation," my values were fashioned much after the patterns that were used in their upbringing as well. I must acknowledge that my granddaughter is being raised very much the way her mother was. She is being given high moral guidelines, and if/when she strays, she is reminded and redirected accordingly.

> When you are guided by the Holy Spirit you need no longer obey Jewish laws. But when you follow your own wrong inclinations, your lives will produce these evil results: impure thoughts, eagerness for lustful pleasure ... hatred and fighting, jealousy and anger, constant effort to get the best for yourself, complaints and criticisms, the feeling that everyone else is wrong except those in your little group—and there will be wrong doctrine, envy, murder, drunkenness, wild parties, and all that sort of thing. But when the Holy Spirit controls our lives, he will produce this kind of fruit in us: love, joy, peace, patience, kindness, goodness, faithfulness, gentleness and self-control; and here there is no conflict with Jewish laws. (Galatians 5:18–21 TLB)

The Galatian letter was intended to guide these new Christians into a *new truth*. Jesus's sacrifice superseded all the laws laid down in the Jewish religion. Before Jesus's ministry on earth, Gentiles were excluded from the worship of the One True God. One of the reasons the religious leaders of the time sought to eliminate Jesus was because of His efforts to save *all* humankind. He was bringing the truth to *even these*, as opposed to limiting them to following Jewish laws and customs.

Paul reminded the people of Galatia that if left up to their own innate wills, the results would be evil—impure thoughts, eagerness for lustful pleasure, hatred and fighting, jealousy and anger, constant effort to get the best for yourself, complaints, and criticisms. The result I think I can most identify with is "the feeling that everyone else is wrong except those in your little group" (Galatians 5:20 TLB). Can you identify with this? "The feeling that everyone else is wrong except those in [my] little group" (Galatians 5:20 TLB). Hmmm. First of all, I have rarely had "my little group" in life. I have rarely been a joiner because I think I am too independent a thinker. I was raised by a father who had very distinct opinions on many issues and situations in life. He could be very vocal regarding those opinions. It didn't matter whether it was a next-door neighbor, a school principal, or a pastor/priest. Dad would exercise his right of free speech and give his opinion. Dad was excommunicated from the Roman Catholic Church because he had an adverse opinion regarding birth control.

We started attending a Protestant church because my mother insisted that we "go to church *somewhere*" when I became old enough to either make my First Holy Communion or begin going to Sunday school. The decision was for our family to attend and eventually join one of the Protestant churches in our Queens, New York City, neighborhood.

Drunkenness, wild parties … Fortunately, these conditions have never been a part of the lives of anyone in our family. We haven't been teetotalers, but except for less-than-a-handful number of incidents with alcohol consumption, we have managed to lead a legitimately sober lifestyle. I know that I have been excluded from being invited to go out with colleagues either after work or on the weekends for fellowship and drinking. I have listened as there have been stories told about the fun times that have been had. Would I condemn the behavior? No, I wouldn't, but I just see fun from a different vantage point. Being out of control and feeling sick as an aftereffect just doesn't seem like something that would interest me. "Drunkenness, wild parties (Galatians 5:21 TLB), and all that sort of thing" don't suit me, but I am led to believe that Jesus may have found Himself there with my associates, just as I believe He was in His time on earth. Jesus was known to lecture His critics as they tried to condemn Him for hanging out with the tax collectors of His time. Jesus said, "It is not the healthy who need a doctor, but the sick. But go and learn what this means: 'I desire mercy, not sacrifice.' For I have not come to call the righteous, but sinners" (Matthew 9:12–13 NIV). He was there among them, because it was with them He wanted to share the answers to questions and lifestyles that could lead them to eternal life with Him and the Father. Jesus I'm sure wouldn't have gotten drunk, but He loved them and wanted the best for those whom He cared about and kept company with.

"When you are guided by the Holy Spirit ..." (Galatians 5:18 TLB). At sixteen years of age, I accepted Christ into my heart as my personal Savior. I've already shared my story with you. But it didn't stop there. As I've lived my life, as I have grown older, as I've continued to mature in my faith, I've become more and more intentional in my walk with Christ. I believe that I can be led by the Holy Spirit.

"When the Holy Spirit controls our lives, he will produce this kind of fruit in us: love, joy, peace, patience, kindness, goodness, faithfulness, gentleness and self-control" (Galatians 5:22–23 TLB). Wow! What an epitaph that sentence could create! "Rick Schin, known to show love, joy, peace, patience, kindness, goodness, faithfulness, gentleness, and self-control." Not bad, right? You see, on my own, I really stand little chance of being able to model these fine characteristics. Let's try to look at some of these elements individually.

Love: what is it? First Corinthians 13 is known as "The Love Chapter." Above all things, Paul writes, "There are three things ... faith, hope, and love—and the greatest of these is love" (1 Corinthians 13:13 TLB).

Joy: This is something I believe only a relationship with Jesus Christ can acquire for us. No matter what our circumstances, Jesus can provide us with joy. Please try not to confuse joy with happiness. Who knows what being happy really means? We are directed to the word *contentment,* which involves satisfaction. The formal definition of joy is in part "a feeling of great pleasure and happiness" (Google.com/searchjoy). Even if the world as we know it is crashing down around us, we may experience joy, because of the love of Christ in our lives. Surrendering to Christ will put us in a position to be joyful. Just knowing that Jesus has my back allows me to be joyful, even if my world is falling apart around me. Happiness can be an elusive thing, and at times I've found it to be short-lived. Joy is consistent and can be experienced whatever happens. The Bible says, "The joy of the Lord is your strength" (Nehemiah 8:10 NLT) so I believe we should partner with the Holy Spirit and welcome "the joy of the Lord." His strength will carry us successfully through life's ups and downs, continuing to provide us God's joy!

Peace: The accepted definition of peace is "freedom from disturbance; quiet and tranquility; a state or period in which there is no war or a war has ended" (Google.com/searchpeace). Literally for millennia, the world has tried to arrive at a time of peace. Our nation can't even reach a point of internal peaceful coexistence. Sadly, there are too many homes unsuccessfully searching for the element known as "peace." At the start of my wedding ceremony, everyone heard the words "In sickness and in health, in good times and bad … until death do us part." Other couples say these words too. Thereafter begs the question "Will they become part of a terrible statistic, where the percentage of couples who marry will divorce 50 percent of the time?" The lack of peace in the home can be blamed on or attributed to many things: abuse (and that's food for a wholly different book!), financial challenges, infidelity, and too many others to list. In a biblical sense, peace may be described as totality or completeness, success, fulfillment, wholeness, harmony, or security and well-being. All of these definitions make us want to attain as high a quantity as we can of this elusive entity called *peace*.

Patience: Occasionally, I used to joke to my students, if they were getting off-task, "Look, I'm like a doctor going out of business. I'm losing my patients!" *(Patience*—get it?) So the world's definition of patience is "the capacity to accept or tolerate delay, trouble, or suffering without getting angry or upset" (Google.com/searchpatience). The apostle Paul writes to the church at Ephesus and all Christians everywhere, "Be patient with each other, making allowance for each other's faults because of your love" (Ephesians 4:2 TLB). "Without getting angry or upset … making allowance for each other's faults …" (Ephesians 4:2 TLB). OK then!

Neither of these definitions is easy. My mortal self is not naturally directed to pulling off either of these. I'd like to see them as part of my epitaph, yes! But I can't do it alone! I need help, and I know where to get it. With Christ's help, I might come close to showing patience. Grace might be another word for patience.

Kindness: A dictionary definition of kindness is "the quality of being friendly, generous, and considerate" (Google.com/searchkindness). In Luke 6:35, we read, "Love your *enemies!* Do good to *them!* Then your reward from heaven will be great, and you will truly be acting as sons of God: for he is kind to the *unthankful* and to those who are *very wicked*" (Luke 6:35 TLB). Have you ever known anyone who was *truly wicked?* We have all either experienced interaction with or seen the practices of the wicked. The Word of God instructs us to "love [our] *enemies!* [For us to] do good to *them!*" (Luke 6:35 TLB). Why? Because "Then [our] reward from heaven will be great, and [we] will truly be acting as sons [and daughters] of God: for he is kind to the *unthankful* and to those who are *very wicked*" (Luke 6:35 TLB). Now before we get all nervous and jerky here, let's dissect this a bit. "[God] is kind to the *unthankful* and to those who are *very wicked*" (Luke 6:35 TLB). I will say if it's good enough for God, it's good enough for me! Likewise, I'd be lax if I didn't admit that I've been an *unthankful* person a few times in my lifetime. How glad I am that God was kind to the *unthankful* me in those times. We should follow the Golden Rule more often. "Do for others what you want them to do for you" (Matthew 7:12 TLB). I'd like to think that there have been no times where I was wicked, but I am so glad that God has loved me and was kind during those times when I displayed *anything but* Christlike behavior. I hope I don't have any enemies, but for me to achieve God's goal, with God's help, through the power of the Holy Spirit, I may love them and *do good to them*.

Goodness: Galatians 6:9 (TLB) reads, "And let us not get tired of doing what is right, for after a while we will reap a harvest of blessing if we don't get discouraged and give up." The dictionary definition of goodness is "the quality of being morally good or virtuous; a belief in the basic goodness of mankind" (Google.com/searchgoodness). We don't know what we may experience from people at first glance. Only after we've spent some time with them can we get to know which way their moral compass really points. I tend to think that our natural instinct is to at first trust the folks we meet. Children seem to naturally get along with each other. Typically, children don't see racial, physical, or cultural differences in other children. It's only after adults or older children have the opportunity to alter their behaviors that children begin discriminating against others.

We've outlined some important traits to live by to successfully get along with others. No one has said that attaining this lifestyle is going to be easy. But anything worth doing isn't guaranteed to be *easy*. Here is where a faith in and dependency on Christ comes into play. Christ will lead us to reach levels of acceptance to Him, and our contributions to society will also contribute to Christ's kingdom here on earth. People will want to follow Christ and His model for living.

Reflection: Do you balk at the idea that you won't be in total control of your life? Is it your belief that you *know it all* and there isn't any situation that you cannot handle by yourself? Well, the truth is that Christian living is all about *giving up control* of your life to the power and judgment of Jesus Christ. The good news is that the Holy Spirit will guide you through each day. Stop fighting, and make a decision for Christ *today!*

DON'T GRIEVE THE HOLY SPIRIT

Ephesians 4:25–32

To grieve means to feel sorrow for or because of or to cause great stress to someone (Google.com/searchgrieve). I think sometimes in general conversation, we misuse the word *grief*. I'm to blame for some of this. It's not uncommon for me to very glibly say, *"Good grief! Get over it!"* The "it" is probably something trivial in *my* opinion, but if not crucial to anyone's existence, it's at least important to the someone I am criticizing. First of all, I can't think of anything good about grief! So maybe the expression *"Good grief!"* is really an oxymoron. Good and grief contradict each other.

When it comes to the scripture passage above, Paul gets very specific about what actions will give the Holy Spirit grief. I'll list some very bad or inappropriate/unacceptable behavior for the believer and at least antisocial behavior by those who don't know Christ as their Savior. We'll highlight and drill down on some of those less understood behavior characteristics and simply mention those more universally known in society.

Here goes! The Bible verses will be taken from The Living Bible paraphrase. In verse 25, Paul flat-out states, "Stop lying to each other; tell the truth, for ... when we lie to each other we are hurting ourselves" (Ephesians 4:25 TLB). Telling the truth as a matter of consistency creates in us a wonderfully special condition among people that keeps life so simple. Whatever you tell me, I will take as completely true and we can more easily do business or even just enjoy each other's company. A great example of this was when my wife and I bought our house. Because I knew the seller through an affiliation with my dad, the seller and I agreed to a selling price, and we *shook hands on it*. Interestingly enough, when Lee Ann and I went to the lender to fill out a mortgage application, the man said, "Where's your sales agreement?" I responded that we didn't have one. He asked me how we had made the deal. The reply I gave him was "We *shook on it.*" That handshake suited the seller and me just fine; we trusted our truthful word and each other. As far as Mr. Schomer and I were concerned, nothing more was needed nor had to be said about it. Unfortunately, just to finish the story, Mr. Schomer and I had to draw up and sign a sales agreement for us to complete the mortgage application. You can see that the human condition right now has become degraded to where a person's word is not commonly accepted as it had been in the past. I found working with teenagers that I couldn't automatically accept their statements as the truth, because too many times the kids were, simply put, lying to me. What a very sad commentary that is for this younger generation. I had to apologize to the "good kids," those who were being truthful with me, and explain to them that I felt their lives would be so much more complex going forward, because they weren't going to be able to accept the statements of others as being truthful at face value. They will always be expected to *prove* everything—have physical evidence. So sad.

Paul wrote to the people of Ephesus, "Stop being mean-tempered and angry" (Ephesians 4:31 TLB). The apostle noted that anger is usually associated with a *hot temper.* I must confess that as a young person I had a hot temper. If something didn't go my way, I would seclude myself until I'd be able to handle the situation. One day, when I was still living at home with my parents (I can't remember what it was), I didn't agree with something my mother told me to do. Because I was hot-tempered, as I walked out to the car, I threw my keys! Yes, I threw the keys into a big, jagged, spiny, stickily bush! I *showed her* how I felt about what she wanted me to do! Yeah, I *showed her all right*; the keys flew deep into that big, jagged, spiny, stickily bush, and it took me a considerable amount of time crawling around under and eventually in it before I found the keys. Stupid! Stupid! Stupid! All because of my hot temper. My anger put me in a bad position.

The irrational part about losing your temper is that you also *lose control of yourself.* Sometimes, people do awful things when they lose control and their temper takes over the situation. I'm guessing that Satan enjoyed the argument I had with my mom, and then I am equally certain that he laughed the whole time I crawled around looking for the car keys.

By the time I returned home from wherever I'd been going, Mom and I were over whatever the argument had been about. But this doesn't always work with anger. Oftentimes, the anger carries on for long periods of time. I could've come home still angry, my mom might've still been upset, and the whole thing could've become a tinderbox. Paul warns in his letter to the Ephesians, "Don't sin by nursing your grudge. Don't let the sun go down with you still angry—get over it quickly; for when you are angry you give a mighty foothold to the devil: (Ephesians 4:26–27 TLB).

In the letter to the Ephesians, Paul discusses how we are supposed to talk as Christians. He writes, "Don't use bad language. Say only what is good and helpful to those you are talking to, and what will give them a blessing" (Ephesians 4:29 TLB). *Isn't this interesting?* Have you ever thought about what your conversations with others might *mean* to those you talk with? Do you have different conversations with other Christians than with unbelievers? What is your overall conduct like between the two? "Don't use bad language. Say only what is good and helpful to those you are talking to ..." (Ephesians 4:29 TLB). Something that comes to mind for me here is how we look at and describe "bad language." Certainly, there are various ways to describe what may be considered to be "bad language." We might be talking about "foul language." "Foul language" is too often used by very well-educated individuals as well as folks who are not highly schooled. Also, foul language occurs because people have heard and consequently used socially unacceptable vocabulary words as a result of a greatly limited word command. In other words, they can't help it. Their environment has been such that they think nothing of using profanity regardless of who may be there to hear them. As an aside, over the years, I have counseled my students to beware of using off-colored language *in general*, because there are certainly times when we wouldn't want a word to slip out in mixed company (people who swear a lot and those who rarely do so).

"Say only what is good and helpful to those you are talking to, and what will give them a blessing" (Ephesians 4:29 TLB). Have you ever had a conversation with someone and later thought about it? With your thoughts, did you think about whether or not your talk had given "them a blessing?" In truth, I can't recall ever having done so. But I would like to conduct myself that way in the future! How cool that would be! What a goal to have. "Say only what is good and helpful to those you are talking to, and what will give them a blessing" (Ephesians 4:29 TLB). I want to give people blessings when and wherever I can. We can only imagine a world where people "say only what is good and helpful to those [they] are talking to, and … give them a blessing" (Ephesians 4:29 TLB). Jackie Gleason might've said, *"How sweet it is!"*

I knew a man years ago named Norvell (not his real name). Norvell has been deceased for quite a number of years. One day Norvell shared one of his many treasured wisdoms with me, which I have since put into practice. He told me, "If you want to be treated really well, for instance, at the bank, the grocery store, or if you're out to dinner, make it a point to compliment those who work there. Lay it on thick. Be sure they know how much you appreciate their *good service* and that you can see how hard they are working. If this is a place where you go a lot, in the future, when you ask them to do something for you, they will treat you like a king." I have employed this technique, and I have found Norvell's advice to be sound. I go to a reasonable number of conferences and large sit-down dinners as a township commissioner. As I watch the servers taking great pride in what they are doing, I am always very deliberate about thanking the servers for all their hard work and great service. I tell them, "Thank you for doing such a good job here tonight." This always brings a smile to their faces. The other day, I thanked a man at the grocery store for collecting the carts from the parking area, as patrons leave them for him to gather and organize. Do you how know he responded? He said, "Thank you so much for saying that!" I know I made his day. I am practicing what Paul wrote about to the Ephesians. "Say only what is good and helpful to those you are talking to, and what will give them a blessing" (Ephesians 4:29 TLB). Doing this is not difficult. And honestly, I walk away with a blessing as well.

So now to the theme of this book section. Ephesians 4:30 reads, "Don't cause the Holy Spirit sorrow by the way you live" (Ephesians 4:30 TLB). Paul went on. "Quarreling, harsh words, and dislike of others should have no place in your lives" (Ephesians 4:31 TLB). We've all met people who seem to revel in the thought of being at odds with all who come in contact with them. These people always seem to be unhappy about something! And they don't mind your knowing it. So getting into a quarrel with them just seems to be par for the course. It's just what they do. OK, now that we know their MO, what're we gonna do about it? Well, Paul has the antidote for this diseased behavior. Paul directs, "Be kind to each other, tenderhearted, forgiving one another … [and here's the oomph we need to get this done in reality] just as God has forgiven you, because you belong to Christ" (Ephesians 4:32 TLB). None of us can carry out Paul's plans on our own. And what's more, I can assure you that you won't pull it off every chance you get. You *will* slip up; it's gonna happen. To have any chance at all to be true to Paul's instructions for the Ephesians and us, we must appeal to Jesus and the Holy Spirit. In the beginning of the day, ask God to manage your day so that you can be a good, successful person. Earlier in the book, we spoke about having grace in our lives. Paul's words stand out to me as being equated to having and giving away grace through our actions. "[Being] kind to each other, tenderhearted, forgiving one another" (Ephesians 4:32 TLB) will be a blessing to us and the people we meet, but the Holy Spirit should smile on us for this action as well. When we behave in this way, we can be sure that we won't "cause the Holy Spirit sorrow by the way [we] live" (Ephesians 4:30 TLB).

Just to recap here, ways not to cause the Holy Spirit sorrow or grieving include avoiding the following:

- lying; this is hurtful to ourselves and others
- becoming uncontrollably angry; don't stay angry, and get over it quickly
- using bad language; say only good things and be a blessing to others
- being mean and bad-tempered; do not use harsh words, quarreling, or developing a dislike for others and instead be kind, tenderhearted, and forgiving of each other

Grieving the Holy Spirit is a serious matter. We should make every effort to invite the Holy Spirit to be with us every minute of every day, so that we can actually be authentic in our goal. Don't grieve the Holy Spirit.

Reflection: Have you grieved the Holy Spirit? (Be honest with yourself and then with God by taking a serious look at your recent life's actions.) *Immediately* ask God for His forgiveness.

LIVING FOR JESUS: WHAT OUR ATTITUDES SHOULD BE (YOU KNOW—THE BE-ATTITUDES?)

Matthew 5:1–12

So Jesus went up on a hill near a place called Capernaum with his twelve disciples to possibly get some rest. Jesus was becoming almost rockstar-like for his time. Masses of followers were crowding to see and hear him preach. Well, why wouldn't they? Jesus was healing the sick, raising people from the dead, and generally just bringing the prospects of hope to those who essentially had none under the society ruled by an exclusive power group— the elite Jewish class of that day. But even the everyday Jew was being persecuted under the harsh rule of an exclusive few—religious tyrants who were *large and in charge,* if you get my drift. There were so many rules and regulations that the common person couldn't possibly begin to follow or obey them. It could be said that the fundamental rules of God had morphed into a religion dictated by men who made up the rules as they went along. Sure, there were God's laws, but so much of the Judaism of Jesus's time became convoluted and warped. About the only people who could follow the rules, follow the law were those religious leaders in control. But then they really had nothing else to do but look pious and *obey the rules.* Even these leaders were supported by the general public through monetary contributions to the temple. It wasn't a very pretty picture. Jesus entered the scene to get things back to how *God intended* things to be in the first place.

What really rankled the religious leaders was that Jesus opened things up to the general public who then *were included* for a change. Jesus showed the people that God loved *all people*, not just the Jews. This is what led to the death of Jesus Christ.

Well anyway, the beatitudes—the message from Jesus on the mountain—may be interpreted as being promises from God to those who believe in and live for Christ. They are wonderful promises. There are eight of these in all. They cover a wide distribution of gifts to those who accept and believe in the power given to Christ followers. It's important to understand that being blessed can happen even during times of hardship. Blessing should not imply happiness. Maybe joy, but not necessarily happiness; we've discussed this difference earlier in the book. I'll admit we typically associate blessings with joyful occurrences, but it will build our faith and beliefs in Jesus if we can look for and find blessings in *everything* that happens to us. If we believe in the King of Kings and Lord of Lords, and the Lord of *all*, our faith in God's will and love for us will allow us to accept whatever God permits for us in our lives. To me, Job represents the type of follower I want to emulate in my walk with Christ. Job lost his possessions, his children, and his health. Not understanding the whys of all these happenings, Job continued to believe in and follow the will of God. Job demonstrates for us that whether God allows blessing or suffering to come to us, even though testing while in this world sometimes is difficult, the results while *enduring* often creates a deeper relationship with God. Great rewards will come in the end to those who endure. Praise God!

OK, buckle your seatbelt. Here we go!

"Blessed are the poor in spirit, for theirs is the kingdom of heaven" (Matthew 5:3 NIV). In The Living Bible, the verse reads, "Humble men are very fortunate! For the Kingdom of Heaven is given to them" (Matthew 5:3 TLB). Humility is not a trait easily practiced. I hope that I have gotten better at this, because I know that in my younger days, I didn't always display humble behavior. I was very fortunate as a young boy growing up in Queens. We belonged to a church where the organist/choir director was a lady who had graduated from the Julliard School in New York City and had written and published music. She took an interest in my singing. She even gave me free, private voice lessons. Well, I often sang solos in church. Here's where the lack of humility comes in. After church, I made sure that

I walked *up the stairs* where many church attendees would be *walking down and exiting*, just so that they could tell me how well I'd sung that day in the services. Not very humble behavior!

So what does being humble get for the man? The Bible says, "Humble men are very fortunate, for the Kingdom of Heaven is given to them" (Matthew 5:3 TLB). The kingdom of heaven *is theirs*! What would it be like to be the recipient of the kingdom of heaven? It is written in the Bible that when Jesus ascended into heaven, His disciples were left with powers here on earth.

> And … he told them, "You are to go into the world and preach the Good News to everyone, everywhere." And those who believe [in Jesus] shall use my authority to cast out demons … and they will be able to place their hands on the sick and heal them. (Mark 16:15–18 TLB)

We know there are those people who do have "the healing touch." They aren't always doctors either. I have been treated by medical professionals who are Christians. It is terrific when you can know they believe, because they will treat you knowing where the healing power comes from. Because it's God who does the healing, it doesn't have to be a Christian doctor treating you, but it's an added dimension when the doc is a believer. I'm not 100 percent certain about exactly what the *kingdom of heaven* is, but I believe in the Mark 16 account of Christ's commission to His followers right before He left earth. "Go into the world and preach the Good News to everyone, everywhere. Use my authority to cast out demons … and place [your] hands on the sick and heal them" (Mark 16:15–18 TLB). I believe that committed Christians today may have the *authority* to do the same things!

Many years ago, I took a course written by Bruce Bugbee and Don Cousins, titled Network, where I was able to have my spiritual gifts identified and confirmed. One of the gifts was the gift of teaching, which transformed the last eighteen years of my life. I have shared that another of my spiritual gifts is the gift of intercessory prayer. You've read here in the book about what I think prayer can do in a person's life. Some people have the gift of healing. They can place their hands on the sick and heal them.

It happens! I have seen it happen! Is this *the only way* God heals people? No. Oh, and by the way, we wrote earlier about *miracles*. I've been a part of another miracle: a healing! A friend's wife had pancreatic cancer. They are both Christians, fierce believers and followers of Christ, and they believe in the power of prayer. There were many Christians all over the world praying for the wife's healing. I prayed for a year for this woman. She went through such a difficult time with the cancer itself and the known remedies to destroy it. She underwent a critical prescribed surgical procedure, and voila! It was successful! Praise God! Glory to God! The doctors were blown away by how the healing had taken place. My friend reported that the medical staff said they had never seen anything like it! I wasn't present while talking with the doctors, but my friend testified before them about how his wife was healed. He gave all the glory to God, where it belonged.

"Blessed are those who mourn, for they will be comforted" (Matthew 5:4 NIV). In The Living Bible, the verse reads, "Those who mourn are fortunate! For they shall be comforted" (Matthew 5:4 TLB). I think sometimes that when we read this particular beatitude, we can become confused and maybe even conflicted regarding its intentions. I pray for people who have lost loved ones. I record the date of the death, and then I pray regularly for the families and friends for one year. The first year after my mother passed away was very difficult for me to live through. I would observe others living and enjoying life, while I was miserably grieving. *How can they be enjoying themselves—living so happily—while I am feeling so sad and depressed?* I thought. It's understandable. The truth is life goes on. Even after we pass away, those who knew us will grieve, but the rest of the world will keep moving on.

So let's hear the beatitude again. "Blessed are those who mourn, for they will be comforted" (Matthew 5:4 NIV). I have chosen to view this beatitude again as a promise from God. A promise! I've said that I like to pray within God's Word. My prayer becomes "Blessed are the friends and family [of the deceased person's name] who mourn, for they will be comforted." "For they *will* be comforted" is where the promise really takes hold for me. I then go on to pray, "And may the friends and family *recognize this promised blessing and experience the promised comfort.*" I have been prone to pray a blessing on the mourners, but don't you see? The beatitude *promises* the blessing! That's right. It's *already there* in the promise. Those who are grieving the death of a lost one *are blessed*. Jesus promised it. So from there, I pray that as time passes, those who are grieving will *recognize this comfort*. Amen.

In another sense, this same beatitude can have a broader meaning. Since I am not a Bible scholar, even though I write with the authority entrusted in me as a practicing Christian, I do examine the meaning and interpretation of God's Word.

The entire New Testament of the Holy Bible is explained through The Daily Study Bible Series written by William Barclay, a twentieth-century Church of Scotland minister. Dr. Barclay was also a radio and television presenter. In The Daily Study Bible Series's *The Gospel of Matthew Volume 1*, Barclay explains his study and understanding of Matthew 5:4. Barclay writes that one receives a blessing as one endures the "bitterest sorrow that life can bring." He goes on to write, "The Arabs have a proverb: 'All sunshine makes a desert.'" "The land on which the sun always shines will soon become an arid place in which no fruit will grow" (The Daily Study Bible Series's *The Gospel of Matthew Volume 1*).

Another interpretation of this beatitude takes into consideration a person's mourning about the type of life that has been led. A sincere person will mourn over the sin that has been in his life. I might reword the scripture verse to read, "Those who mourn *over sin* are fortunate, for they shall be comforted." The comfort comes as we confess our sins to God, and His forgiveness of those sins brings the comfort. I'm sure I can identify my sins on a daily basis. Just because I profess Jesus Christ as my personal Savior doesn't mean that I have gracious, sin-free living all under control. Far be that situation! I've heard it said, "Christians aren't perfect. They're just forgiven." I say, "Amen!" to that.

"Blessed are the meek, for they will inherit the earth" (Matthew 5:5 NIV). In The Living Bible, the verse reads, "The meek and lowly are fortunate! For the whole world belongs to them" (Matthew 5:5 TLB). OK, I looked up the definition of *meek* (Google.com/searchmeek). It was just as I thought: "quiet, gentle, and easily imposed on; submissive." I don't suppose that I would oppose being described as quiet or gentle. There certainly is room for soft, low, inaudibility in our world. Kind, calm, and mild behavior brings smiles to the faces of those I bump into in my travels. But here's the rub. I can't think of anyone I know who would sign up to be "easily imposed on." Consistently being submissive also carries with it a very dark connotation. But Jesus said, "Blessed are the meek, for they will inherit the earth" (Matthew 5:5 NIV). Christ didn't say, "Blessed are the meek, for they *might* inherit the earth," did He? So should we shoot for the blessing in this beatitude? Can you think of anyone you know whom you could honestly describe as having inherited the earth? And what does that look like exactly? What does *to inherit* the earth include? I knew a pastor once who never swore (at least his daughter had never heard him swear in her presence). In fact, he never even used a swear-word alternative. I spent some time in his presence as a boy, and I never heard him even raise his voice in anger. I might use this pastor as the meek example for me. You know, I can think of one other—Christ Himself. And what's more, Christ volunteered for the role. Upon being arrested, he was quiet, gentle, and certainly was imposed on. I think I would be apt to be meek, if I thought I would be able to represent my Lord more accurately by doing so. I have to think that the promised blessing would be worth it! And don't miss this. I'm sure the Holy Spirit would gladly give me the power to be—instead of forceful and maybe obnoxious—meek. I can work on that. We'll see what happens.

"Blessed are those who hunger and thirst for righteousness, for they will be filled" (Matthew 5:6 NIV). In The Living Bible, the verse reads, "Happy are those who long to be just and good, for they shall be completely satisfied" (Matthew 5:6 TLB). While writing this book, I'm not going to kid you or myself. I cannot recall the last time that I *longed* for anything. So I asked *Siri* to clear up the meaning of "to long." The answer? "To have a strong feeling of need or desire for someone or something" (Google.com/search). So now that I understand the question, I'm back to square one. *Have I,* or *when's the last time I* longed for something? I can't remember! How about you? When's the last time you've *longed* for something? Well, you can go ahead and answer that one for yourself.

Jesus preached to and taught those on the mountain that, those who long to be just and good would find happiness. I have written before about the elusive "happiness." I've said that I'm not sure what happiness is, and when we achieve it, I think it's easily lost. I try to dwell on joy, which is longer lasting and can be reached even in difficult times, *if* we depend on the Holy Spirit to guide and direct us. Well anyway, Christ said, "Happy are those who long to be just and good" (Matthew 5:6 TLB). But He didn't just throw it out and just let it hang there, did He? No! Jesus said, "Happy are those who long to be just and good, for they shall be completely satisfied." "For they shall be *completely satisfied*" (Matthew 5:6 TLB). So my dictionary resource indicates that the word *satisfied* may be described as contented and pleased (Google.com/searchsatisfied). Then how can we reach the point of being *satisfied completely*? Jesus says, "Be one of those who long to be just and good" (Matthew 5:6 TLB). Even if a person isn't interested in being a Christian, this would be a terrific way to live. *Long* to be *just* and *good*. I remember the boss at my first management assignment saying, "You need to be firm but fair as you interact with employees and customers." What he was really telling me was to be *just and good* in my dealings. He told me this well before I even thought about getting married and having children. I mention this because in effectively communicating with my wife and certainly parenting my children, this was great advice.

Permit me to take one small detour here. The original translation for this beatitude reads, "Blessed are those who hunger and thirst for righteousness, for they will be filled" (Matthew 5:6 NIV). Being *filled* makes me think about how I feel after a Thanksgiving Day dinner. Leading up to the time of the midday feast, I eat very little. I don't want to spoil my appetite for what I knowingly anticipate to be a wonderful meal! If I have paced myself regarding how much I eat, the result will be my *feeling* and *being filled*. And that is a good and blessed happening. Just one more thing to be said of "Blessed are those who hunger and thirst for righteousness" (Matthew 5:6 NIV). Remember *the blessing is a promise* from our Lord! Accept and depend on it.

"Blessed are the merciful, for they will be shown mercy" (Matthew 5:7 NIV). In The Living Bible, the verse reads, "Happy are the kind and merciful, for they shall be shown mercy" (Matthew 5:7 TLB). *Mercy* is defined as "compassion or forgiveness shown toward someone who it is within one's power to punish or harm" (Google.com/searchmercy). This is all practically, well, self-explainable. Whether or not we have mercy on those we come in contact with is the real issue here. When I struggle to be merciful, when forgiving someone for something, I am drawn to the picture of Christ excruciatingly nailed to and hanging on the cross while saying, "Father, forgive them, for they do not know what they are doing"

(Luke 23:34 NIV). Then I beat myself up over the triviality of my problem with someone whom I cannot seem to forgive! Seemingly, I say to myself, "Really? *Really?* You *can't forgive* this person when the innocent Christ *forgave* those who were unjustly crucifying Him?" So *be forgiving* already! Accept the blessing, be happy, and be merciful. If you do this, you too will be shown mercy. This isn't a case of Karma, but pragmatically I can see how people could look at how we treat others and respond to us in a similar way. Truth be known? I *am* happier being kind than when I am not kind. I've known for years that it's not in my nature to be unkind. I think it's that I was raised by kind, merciful parents, so I typically interact with people in a kindly way. Children probably receive my kindness most often; I can't seem to walk past a baby in a carriage without smiling and waving at the child.

"Blessed are the pure in heart, for they will see God" (Matthew 5:8 NIV). In The Living Bible, the verse reads, "Happy are those whose hearts are pure, for they shall see God" (Matthew 5:8 TLB). Wow! I have a question. How do I get a pure heart? The great theologian William Barclay discusses this beatitude and gets very swiftly to the point. He writes, "[This beatitude] could be translated: *Blessed is the man whose motives are always unmixed, for that man shall see God*" (The Daily Study Bible Series's *The Gospel of Matthew Volume 1*). By "unmixed," Barclay espouses that to truly be in the position to *see God*, our motives would need to be placed so that we aren't looking to *get anything for ourselves* but instead would be looking to please God—to be doing it all for the furtherance of God's kingdom. I don't mean to contradict Jesus, but the Bible tells us, "All have sinned, and come short of the glory of God" (Romans 3:23 NIV). So I must confess that I am finding it almost impossible for *most* people (I won't say *all* people) to receive this "pure heart" blessing. To leave this beatitude positively, I believe it's possible, but only through much intentional, narrow-road behavior, and the leading of the Holy Spirit. So should I accept Barclay's commentary, I will pay closer attention to my intentions in life. I will aim for *unmixed* motives. Maybe then I can be more hopeful regarding a pure heart, being contented, and seeing God.

"Blessed are the peacemakers, for they will be called sons of God" (Matthew 5:9 NIV). In The Living Bible, the verse reads, "Happy are those who strive for peace—they shall be called the sons of God" (Matthew 5:9

TLB). Honestly? It would be so great if I could have written on a cemetery headstone, "Richard F. Schin—Peacemaker." No kidding! How cool would that be? What does it take for a person to get labeled *peacemaker*? "Whataya gotta do to get that handle?" the guy asked. Although I strive to get along with those around me—my neighbors, my professional colleagues, my family, and all others I come in contact with—I can't say that all those folks would necessarily label me *Peacemaker*. In this case, as in others, we need to depend on the assistance of the Holy Spirit. If I'm walking closely behind Him, in His shadow, as I like to think of it, then I *just might* be able to get closer to being considered a peacemaker.

"Blessed are those who are persecuted because of righteousness, for theirs is the kingdom of heaven" (Matthew 5:10 NIV). In The Living Bible, the verse reads, "Happy are those who are persecuted because they are good, for the Kingdom of Heaven is theirs" (Matthew 5:10 TLB). Righteousness is defined as "the quality of being morally right or justifiable" (Google. com/searchmercy). The Living Bible speaks of those who are persecuted "because they are good" (Matthew 5:10 TLB). While attending school in Queens, I was sometimes called a goody-goody because I rarely *(only once)* got into trouble at school. Maybe I can relate to being *persecuted, because I was good*. Kind of like the beatitude about seeing God, I can't wrap my brain around "the Kingdom of Heaven" being mine. Maybe I'll work on being good and let God take care of things the rest of the way.

"Blessed are you when people insult you, persecute you and falsely say all kinds of evil against you because of me. Rejoice and be glad, because great is your reward in heaven, for in the same way they persecuted the prophets who were before you" (Matthew 5:11–12 NIV). In The Living Bible, the passage reads, "When you are reviled and persecuted and lied about because you are my followers—wonderful! Be *happy* about it! Be *very glad!* for a *tremendous reward* awaits you up in heaven. And remember, the ancient prophets were persecuted too" (Matthew 5:11–12 TLB). Right about now, you are thinking, *Has this guy lost it? I've read the book this far, I've agreed and disagreed, I've understood and been confused by some things, but I'm drawing the line here! You're expecting me to feel blessed and/or happy when people dump on me? Really? I guess now I've heard it all!"* OK, don't shut the book yet. It's really not as far off the wall as you might think.

This beatitude is not for consideration if you're a first-time believer still trying to understand your decision for the Lord. Having said that, I shouldn't be so quick to minimize the effectiveness of the newly saved believer. I do recall my witnessing to the student on the bus two days after my getting saved. The boy, Clay, didn't really persecute me; he just kind of looked for a different seat on the bus to escape to. Let's say it this way. When/if you are insulted, perhaps physically abused, lied about (sometimes in really horrible ways), know that these things do not go unnoticed by God. It's hard to do, but the Lord tells us to rejoice and be glad. Clearly, this is something where you will need divine help. "Rejoice and be glad, because great is your reward in heaven" (Matthew 5:12 NIV). Scriptures tell us that heaven is definitely a place where we should look forward to going to. For those who have been treated badly, please note that the conditions in heaven will for sure be a step up, a reward. Now if you are insulted, perhaps physically abused, lied about (sometimes in really horrible ways), please note what Jesus finishes up with "for in the same way they persecuted the prophets who were before you" (Matthew 5:12 NIV). I guess another way to look at this is to say, "You're in good company. The prophets of old were treated just as badly for their beliefs in the Almighty God we serve." Finishing this point (easy to say, less easy to do), be bold in the Lord! Tell others of His goodness and grace. If you are not received well, if you are persecuted for your beliefs, know that your reward is awaiting you in heaven.

As I've thought and written about these beatitudes, it has occurred to me that *I* cannot claim any of these blessings *on my own*. Likewise, I have become convinced that I will be moving in and out of these stages throughout my life. These beatitudes provide ways to be blessed/happy, but human nature can very well stand in the way of our pulling off the behaviors spoken of in these beatitudes. Here is where our faith in the Holy Spirit and His direction of our path comes into play. I am a miserable sinner saved by the grace of God. I can't do anything without Him. I can depend on my God to "never leave nor forsake [me]" (Hebrews 13:5 KJV). Thank You, Jesus.

Reflection: Have you turned as much of your life as you can understand over to Jesus, obviously taking a step-by-step approach (committing the "whole of you" to God that you can genuinely surrender)? Are you experiencing the promises of the beatitudes?

HOW GOD CAN TAKE A WRONG AND MAKE A RIGHT

Genesis 37:1–50:26: The Story of Joseph

You may have heard or read about Joseph and his coat of many colors. Well, Joseph was one of Jacob's twelve sons. As a side note, Jacob is also referred to in the Bible as *Israel*. Because Joseph was the youngest, he was Jacob's *favorite* son. He was hated by his brothers. Maybe you can identify with this story.

An interesting exercise might be to have you *stop,* take a few minutes to reread the story, and *evaluate where you would situate yourself* in this tale about a man and his eleven and one sons. Do you identify with the eleven or relate to the youngest? Put the book down and take a few minutes to reflect on this.

OK, now that you're back, let's continue. If you haven't read the Joseph story as told in Genesis 37:1–50:26, I will attempt to give you a shortened version. Being the youngest sibling can be bad enough, but what happened among Jacob and his sons just added insult to injury, so to speak.

One day, Joseph told his older brothers that he'd had a dream about them all. He claimed that in this dream, the brothers were foreseen as being his subordinates; he would rule over them. I'm sure you can imagine that this *went over like a lead balloon* with them. They were angered by this news, fueling the hatred they had already built up among them. Wait. It doesn't stop there. Joseph had yet another dream, basically using additional symbolism to foretell the same result. This time, even his father was disturbed by what Joseph was telling them. Needless to say, these dreams just fed on the jealousy the brothers had already practiced toward Joseph.

I think it's important to recall Joseph's coat (or robe) of many colors. A typical robe or cloak was a practical part of a person's life tools. It was knee length, short sleeved, *and plain*. Can you see where this is going? Joseph's "fair-haired boy" role was extended even with the cloak/robe/coat of many colors. One more reason for his brothers to jealously hate him.

There came a day, as his brothers were out in the fields tending their father's livestock, when Jacob told his son Joseph to go out to the fields. "See if all is well with your brothers and with the flocks, and bring word back to me" (Genesis 37:14 NIV). Of course, Joseph did as his father directed him. By this time, however, the brothers had grown very jealous and tired of having Joseph continue being the apple of their father's eye. *They decided to kill Joseph.* However, they decided in the end to sell him to traveling merchants for a silver reward. The boys lied to their father Jacob. They had stripped Joseph of his robe, spread goat's blood on it, and told Jacob that Joseph had met a terrible demise. Of course, Jacob had no immediate reason to suspect his sons' dastardly behavior and lies.

Fast-forwarding (you really ought to read the whole story), Joseph was sold again and ended up in the household of the pharaoh of Egypt. It would appear that much significance for Joseph is impacted by dreams. This time, it involved a dream that the pharaoh had, and Joseph was able to explain it to the king's satisfaction and benefit. The pharaoh placed Joseph in charge of the entire kingdom of Egypt! Holy cow! (Hall of Fame New York Yankees player Phil Rizzuto style, right?)

Then there came a famine in Canaan, Joseph's home country. The Egyptians were fine, but Joseph's family were in great danger of not being able to survive. Jacob was old and unable to travel. The brothers made the journey to Egypt to find food for their father and the rest of the family.

Can you even imagine how they must have felt? Remember the brothers sold Joseph into slavery! They actually had fantasized about killing Joseph! Now Joseph was almost king of Egypt! The whole story involves the brothers and Joseph trying to reestablish a relationship and Joseph seeing his father again. Eventually, Joseph revealed himself to his brothers. Of course, they were aghast to discover who the powerful assistant to the pharaoh was—their little brother who had been sold into slavery! On a personal note, I know what kind of an older sibling I was to my six-year-junior brother. Oh, we played games and athletics together, but to my parents' much later surprise, I wasn't always as kind to Donald as I should have been. (Let's just leave it there for now.) Many years later, when I was looking for a job, my little brother Don, a successful business owner, invited me to go to work for him and help him promote his new business. It is a fondly memorable experience for us both.

Upon arriving in Egypt, the brothers realized that Joseph appeared to be in the position of ranking just below the pharaoh, overseeing the kingdom. When his identity had been revealed, Joseph said, "Do not be distressed and do not be angry with yourselves for selling me here, because it was to save lives that God sent me ahead of you" (Genesis 45:5 NIV). It was necessary for me to give you the background, but it is this verse 5 that I want to highlight here. So it would seem that Joseph's brothers were out of the woods on this thing. Not so fast! "What If Joseph holds a grudge against us and pays us back for all the wrongs we did to him?" (Genesis 50:15 TLB). But Joseph said to them, "Don't be afraid. Am I God? You intended me harm, but God intended it for good to accomplish what is now being done, saving of many lives" (Genesis 50:20–21 TLB).

"You intended me harm, but God intended it for good" (Genesis 50:19–20 NIV). This was Joseph's reasoning for forgiving his wicked brothers. Joseph's life was not an easy one. He could have blamed the brothers for all his life's troubles. And he would have had many reasons for doing so! I can't imagine anyone in their right mind finding fault with Joseph if he'd sent his brothers packing—back to his famine-ravaged homeland of Canaan. They did him a horrible injustice! When you think about it, those boys robbed their father of the company of his youngest son too! We can read Joseph's answer to the brothers. "You intended me harm, but God intended it for good" (Genesis 50:19–20 NIV). You see, God was *in* this whole situation.

Life can be strange at times. I can recall how excited I was, at age twenty, to be getting my first *real job*. I was a bank teller. As a bank teller working my way through college, although I really enjoyed the work, I was unable to sustain myself on the meager pay. After graduating from college, the bank offered me a management opportunity. Although I'd wanted to become a teacher, with teaching positions being as scarce as hens' teeth, I decided to take the management offer. What I am leading up to here is that I fully expected to work for that bank for the next forty-five years. Yes, I would work until I was sixty-five years old, retire, get my gold watch and chain and my monthly pension check, receive social security income, and live happily ever after. So let me just tell you it didn't happen that way!

Nope! After a few years, after discovering that life wasn't fair in business sometimes, I quit working at the bank and moved on. Over the following twenty-five years, I worked in sales, office management, and banking again, and I was a business coach.

Why do I mention this, and what does Joseph's story have to do with my career path? Good question! I hesitated to chronicle this. I've thought pretty long and hard about telling it. Well, Joseph was dealt a terrible hand by his brothers. When you read the whole story, you will learn about the twists and turns he endured and overcame throughout his life. I can identify to an extent, but lesser of course, with Joseph and his tale.

There were three times in my business career where, through no fault of my own, I was forced to start all over with a new employer. Can you begin to see a Joseph-Schin comparison developing? Joseph had no control over his situation. During the years when I had gotten back into banking, the financial industry was experiencing major changes. Megabanks were gobbling up smaller, very successful ones, creating layoffs of thousands of employees. Corporate politics ruled the day. I was never good at business politics. When I tell people this, they are often quick to retort, "Come on, Rick, you've been in politics in your township for decades; what do you mean you 'aren't good at politics'?" In my elected position, the voters are my bosses. As long as they are happy with me, I'll continue to get reelected. In the field of corporate politics, I was never good at *reading the tealeaves* or *knowing which way the wind was blowing*. At one establishment, they lost a few funding sources and I needed to leave.

Each time, after briefly sulking and licking my wounds, I took to the pavements and looked for a new job. Let me just say I always knew that God was with and wouldn't abandon me. We (God and I) always found the next *port in the storm* of my journey to the end. Of course, at those times when I'd wanted to stay but couldn't, I'm not going to tell you I was happy about it, but I wasn't afforded much crying time either. I had children, a wife to provide for, and a mortgage to pay.

In my opinion, I was wildly successful in the last nonteaching position I'd held. I have had a difficult time forgiving the boss to whom I tendered an involuntary resignation. If I'd been given the opportunity, I'm very much convinced I could have made up for income shortfalls and stayed on there. The boss didn't have the faith that I had. His loss.

OK! Enough of this slobbering over myself. After that was when my brother Don asked me to join him in his new business. I also began doing some substitute teaching, which ultimately led to the greatest experience a person could ever have in a career! I put my teaching degree to work, extended my own education (I earned a master's degree at age sixty!), and met literally thousands of wonderful young people, their parents, and terrific colleagues! Do you see the Joseph-Schin connection now?

Most of the financial institutions where I worked are no longer in existence. So you see, I wouldn't have been able to continue working with them anyway. At the last bank where I worked, I am receiving a pension for my retirement.

Let me just say the reason for my telling the Joseph-Schin stories is to testify to God's watching out for both Joseph *and* me. In Deuteronomy 31:6 (NIV), Moses wrote, "Be strong and courageous. Do not be afraid or terrified … for the Lord your God goes with you; he will never leave you nor forsake you." The Joseph-Schin story is having a wonderful final few chapters. God never left us; He knew our futures, and as they say these days, "It was *all gooood*."

Reflection: Take a few minutes to evaluate where you would situate yourself in this tale about a man and his twelve sons. Do you identify with the eleven or relate to the younger, and why?

WHERE YOU CAN TURN WHEN LIFE'S STORMS THREATEN

Matthew 8:23–27; Mark 4:35–41; Luke 8:22–25

Everyone has her or his life challenged by adversity at some time. Down through the ages, history has recorded such events and times. Likewise, we can read and discover just how these folks dealt with the storms in their lives. The situations have either made or broken these individuals, based upon how they approached and handled their circumstances. For some, tragedies have been mere bumps in the road, where for others slight inconveniences have appeared to be "the end of the world" for them.

We have three separate biblical accounts of the same incident involving Jesus Christ and His disciples. As an aside, it's examples like this that make the Bible so credible for me. This event was witnessed and experienced by the three gospel writers, but they each tell it just a little bit differently. Have you ever played the game telephone? You know, the child's communication game where several children are selected to directly participate, while the others are considered to be observers? Well anyway, I will explain how the game is played.

All but one of the children are temporarily led to another room, while one of the kids is told a story that she or he will have to tell to the next child in line upon entering the room. Now understand the story, although not necessarily short, has many details that are needed to make the story "work," if you know what I mean. All right, the second child enters the room, and the first child tells the story as she or he recalls it. Well, the process is repeated as many times as there are children to tell and hear it.

Finally, the last kid tells everyone what he heard. You can of course guess the story is *nowhere close* to the original tale.

So the disciples and Jesus were completing a day of ministry when they decided to go to another side of the body of water. They were in the Sea of Galilee. There were mountains surrounding the water. It was not uncommon to experience a sea squall with high winds creating enormous waves, challenging the seaworthiness of vessels caught in the storm. Matthew 8:24 (NIV) tells us, "Without warning, a furious storm came up on the lake ... the waves swept over the boat."

Isn't life this way? If we use the physical event that happened oh so long ago to Jesus as a metaphor, we might be able to relate to their plight by thinking of a time when a fierce emotional "squall" came over us without warning! It might have been something physical or health related or something financial—did you lose a job or get passed over for a promotion that you thought was a sure thing? Was the life storm family oriented—spouse, child, parent? We typically get very short notice prior to these events happening.

Even though some of the disciples were fishermen and accustomed to being on this lake, the surprise of the event threw them off their game. But what I think is interesting is that even with many of the disciples being experienced boatmen, they panicked! Rather than do what should have come naturally to them, they got panicky and called out to Jesus! Ultimately, they really did do the right thing! I get that, but I just find it more than just a little curious. I don't know whether or not they battened down any hatches. Did they try to help themselves? The scriptures do not elaborate on this in any of the accounts of the incident.

Where was Jesus anyway? Verse 24 tells us that "Jesus was sleeping" (Matthew 8:24 NIV). "Jesus was sleeping on a cushion" (Mark 4:38 NIV). Luke recounts, "As they sailed, [Jesus] fell asleep" (Luke 8:23 NIV). Obviously, Jesus was not worried about the trek across the lake. The multitudes were present, making it necessary for the group to go to the other side of the lake; it's very possible that Jesus was exhausted and couldn't help falling asleep, given the chance.

Well, what was Jesus's reaction to the panicking of His disciples? Matthew recalls Jesus responding, "You of little faith, why are you afraid?" (Matthew 8:26 NIV). Mark remembered Jesus saying, "Why are you so afraid? Do you still have no faith?" (Mark 4:40 NIV). Luke recorded Jesus's remark as "Where is your faith?" (Luke 8:25 NIV).

So back at the metaphor, let's think about a storm that either *has* happened or *is* happening now. What is your reaction, and how do you respond when placed under such great pressure? Do you panic and have a melt down?

Jesus came down pretty hard on the disciples' shortness on faith, didn't He? All right, so *what is* faith? "Now faith is being sure of what we hope for and certain of what we do not see" (Hebrews 11:1 NIV). So if we break this down a little, faith is being sure. Sure of what? Sure of what we *hope for.* Faith is believing in God's character. He is who He says He is. We also believe in His promises.

If we're dealing with a real-life, high-intensity storm in our life, as our first reaction to the situation, we should cry out to Jesus! That's right! Jesus and His Holy Spirit *want* to be our "first responders" in the emergencies that creep into our lives. Before the waves come crashing over the bow of your boat (your life), for help in avoiding the high swells (the tremendous emotional strains), seek Jesus; let Him call out to the storm and quiet the winds. He *will* do it!

Reflection: Decide whether or not you will trust in Jesus to allow Him into your current circumstances. You can make a "heavenly 9-1-1 call," so that Jesus and His Holy Spirit *may* be your "first responders" and come to your rescue!

BENEFITS OF CONSTRUCTIVE CRITICISM AND THE TASTE OF HUMBLE PIE

Proverbs 15:31–33 (TLB)

I don't know about you, but being critiqued never really went down well with me. You know how when you've either made something or written something and the person who you showed it to immediately starts telling you how it could've been done differently—or even better!

I mean, come on now. Be honest. Can you really sit there and tell me that you *actually appreciate* this? Really? You're OK with this? Well then, you're a better person than I am.

As much as I have spoken about him—my dad, that is—I can't say that I always appreciated him launching into his "constructive criticism" as often as he did it. Did I ever question Dad's love for me or his genuinely caring motives? No! No, in my heart of hearts, I never felt like he was putting me down. I think Dad felt it almost as though it was his responsibility as a dad to critique me and my work.

Dad was very particular about how my brother and I looked and spoke. He would say, "How you comport yourself will determine how you are received in the world." OK, Schin, *comport*. What in the world is that? Comportment refers to behavior. It includes actions—manners, conduct, demeanor—*and* I believe Dad would have included how we dressed.

So you can see that he saw part of his "dadly responsibility" to be looking at our works with opinions about their credibility. Was this the best we could do in his eyes?

Just so you won't think I'm ragging on my dad, did I eventually appreciate his constructively critical comments? Oh, sure I did! But I wanted him to appreciate my work for the effort and passion that I put into it *first*! Then he could criticize. I must say that I recall his having gotten better at this the older he became.

Solomon writes in Proverbs 15:31–32 (NIV), "If you profit from constructive criticism you will be elected to the wise men's hall of fame. But to reject criticism is to harm yourself and your own best interests." Hmmm. "The wise men's hall of fame." I don't know that Dad acted as he did because of Solomon and his proverbs. I can't even say that he was influenced by anything his immigrant parents necessarily told him. It can certainly be said that he always wanted the best he could provide for his two sons, and whatever he had to honestly do to reach that result he would've done. Dad loved our mom, and they both worked very hard to raise Don and me.

What would it mean to be elected to "the wise men's hall of fame"? How important is *fame*? If we were to ask a hundred people that question, we might get a hundred different answers. When I think of famous people, several individuals come to mind. The two men I want to mention here are so incredibly different, but what they have in common is that they would not have been able to go anywhere in the world without being recognized. Another similarity was that they accomplished fame—and perhaps it could have been a goal of theirs *or not*.

Michael Jackson was a singer, dancer, TV and movie star, and composer. Michael and his family were so very talented musically. He was the featured son and brother because he was the youngest and undeniably *so cute*! The Jackson Five toured the world, giving concerts. We know they eventually hosted their own television show. They were even the voices of a Saturday morning cartoon television show featuring them. At some point, Michael decided to go solo and began recording songs and doing TV specials of his own. Sadly, with this fame came life's complications. Like so many other stars of entertainment, Michael became ensnared and blinded by the lights and succumbed to an excess of his vices. His music will live on, but his legacy has been tainted by his *comportment*.

The Rev. Dr. Billy Graham was a pastor, author, evangelist, and Christian. Billy Graham traveled the world professing the love and saving power of Jesus Christ! Movies were sponsored in his name. He actually made cameo appearances in them. Lives were eternally altered because of these movies—this author being one of those lives! Unlike other well-known evangelists, Billy did not organize and form a university named after himself. Jesus Christ was always the focus of his crusades. He would pack the largest stadiums all across the United States and around the world. Billy Graham delivered sermons from the texts of biblical scripture; he told the truth, kept the message simple, and people responded to his invitations. No, to *God's* invitations. Dr. Graham lived a long, satisfying life. His legacy resonates among those such as this author and millions of others who've accepted the free gift of salvation from their sins. Franklin Graham and his sister have carried the torch first lit by Dr. Graham, and Christ's message continues to be declared around the world. The legacy of the Rev. Dr. Billy Graham remains positive and intact.

So fame can be a blessing or a curse, can't it? If I were to acquire fame while comparing the two famous people above, I know which course I would like to choose.

But the fame that Solomon speaks of is a *wise fame*. In fact, Solomon writes about "the wise men's hall of fame" that we could be elected to if we can "profit from constructive criticism" (Proverbs 15:31–32 TLB). It stands to reason that unless and until I would permit myself to accept Dad's constructive criticism, any available wisdom would be lost for me.

Let's go the extra mile here. "But to reject criticism is to harm yourself and your best interests" (Proverbs 15:32 TLB). I will tell you that I know my dad always had *my best interests* at heart as he critiqued my efforts. He could be brutally honest with me at times, but he was just doing what he could to make me better in the end. Again, was he a pawn of Solomon's theories? I can't say, but after the fact, I can see the *wisdom* in it all.

"Humility and reverence for the Lord will make you both wise and honored" (Proverbs 15:33 TLB). For me, humility enters my thoughts as I meet a former student somewhere in a public place and they honor me by going out of their way to stand and chat with me for a few minutes or when I see their Facebook page pop up if I reach out to them and post a comment. When they respond, I am humbled.

This is a very pragmatic approach, one that I can certainly wrap my head around. The world's definition of *humble* reads, "Having or showing a modest or low estimate of one's own importance" (Google.com/searchhumble). The opposite of *humble* is *proud* or *overbearing*.

Proud. This isn't the *proud* that we feel when we watch our children do well in a school concert or when they participate in a sporting event. Or even when they get accepted to the college, university, or trade school of their choice, or certainly how proud we are of them when they get their first real job. No, that *proud* shows what I'm calling *positive, healthy pride*. I realize that even this can get out of control and come across as overbearing. This type of *proud* is defined as "having or showing a high or excessively high opinion of oneself or one's importance" (Google.com/searchproud). It's this type of pride that is so often what we have to put up with in the company we keep. Other words being associated with this version of *proud* are arrogant, conceited, vain, self-important, or full of oneself. I once had a boss who continually bragged about her high school-aged son. I could tolerate the accolades she verbally adorned him with, but what I finally got truly sickened by was her bragging about how *tall he had gotten!* Really? Being tall is not an accomplishment! It's all in the genes (spoken like a true vertically challenged man, right?).

"Humility and reverence for the Lord will make you both wise and honored" (Proverbs 15:33 TLB). If we can avoid pride while at the same time showing deep respect for God, wisdom and honor are attainable for us.

Reflection: What might you do to keep in check the temptation to constructively criticize those you come in contact with (your spouse, children, coworkers, employees, et al.)? Could you look at and appreciate their accomplishments *before* you begin critiquing them? Have you encountered the *proud person* in your travels? What was your response? Did you participate in a "Can You Top This?" competition, or were you able to follow the model provided in proverbs? "Humility and reverence for the Lord will make you both wise and honored" (Proverbs 15:33 TLB).

PETER'S ACTIONS, HOW JESUS ACCEPTED THEM, AND WHAT THAT MEANS TODAY TO US

Luke 22:25–34, 54–62

Peter was greatly indignant and insulted by Jesus's prediction about how he would react to the arrest of Jesus. Hearing Christ tell of how He would be arrested, tried as a criminal, and brutally put to death—*crucified*—Peter spoke up persuasively, as recorded in Luke 22:33 (NIV). "Lord, I am ready to go to jail with you, and even to die with you."

Jesus responded, "Peter, let me tell you something. Between now and tomorrow morning when the rooster crows, you will deny me three times, declaring that you don't even know me" (Luke 22:34 TLB). That retort from Jesus had to have been *crushing* to Peter.

Peter may have been the most outspoken of the twelve apostles in Jesus's ministry on earth. He certainly became one of the boldest witnesses for the faith. His beginnings were certainly humble in origin. He was born about 1 BC and died sometime around AD 67. As an aside, Peter's death came about 1,900 years before my graduation from high school (1967).

Peter was ready *even to die with Jesus* if necessary, right? Peter was among the first disciples called by Jesus, and he was frequently their spokesman—for good or bad. One thing that he is credited with is the special insight that he had concerning Jesus's identity. In Luke 9:20 (NIV), we learn that Peter was the first to call Jesus the Son of the Living God—the Christ. When Jesus called him, Peter knew that He was of God and

82

felt unworthy to be in Jesus's presence (Luke 5:6–8). Even so, Jesus did not hesitate and told Peter and his brother Andrew that He would make them "fishers of men" (Mark 1:17 NIV).

A casual, occasional acquaintance with Jesus was not what Peter thought their relationship to be. That's why I believe Peter vowed his allegiance even unto death, if necessary. In fact, Peter was the only disciple to follow (all be it at a safe distance behind) Jesus after His arrest in the garden of Gethsemane. We might make reference here to the event that really makes Peter stand out in my view. It's when Peter walked on the water, as he was commanded to do by Jesus as a testament to his faith (Matthew 14:25–32 TLB). As long as Peter focused on Christ, he was able to walk on top of the lake. It was only when Peter "saw the wind, he was afraid and, beginning to sink, cried out, 'Lord save me!'" (Matthew 14:30 NIV).

Peter was bold but oftentimes in the wrong. Jesus loved the disciples and knew which of those would remain loyal to Him and those who would betray Him (Judas Iscariot). Peter was an eyewitness to the many miracles that Jesus did. Along with John and James, Peter shared in experiencing the Transfiguration of Christ. This was where Jesus's humanity was unwrapped to reveal the glory of His divinity (Matthew 17:1–9 NIV).

So what does any of this mean to you and me today? You know, Peter was what we might call aggressive when it came to his following of the Lord. *But* he crumpled when his well-being was challenged during the last days of Christ's life, right before His crucifixion. Peter displayed *his humanity* under pressure. What we might say in modern terms is he choked.

Who wouldn't? Consider the scene. For three years, you've lived with a man whom you believed to be sent directly by God Himself. You have pledged your loyalty to Him. "Lord, I am ready to go to jail with you, and even to die with you" (Luke 22:33 TLB) is what you boasted about *just hours before His violent arrest.* One of the participants accompanying the soldiers arresting Jesus had his ear amputated and Jesus restored it *right before your very eyes!* Now in order to be true in keeping with the boasting you'd done at supper, you have followed your Messiah, Jesus. Yes, followed, then to three times, having been identified with Jesus, you have denied *even knowing Him.* Jesus's predictive words come to ring in your ears as a reminder.

Jesus did not rebuke Peter. He foretold Peter's eventual actions, but Christ did not fault Peter. In fact, we are told (Mark 16:1–7) that when the women went to the tomb with the embalming spices where the body of Jesus was laid, they met an angel. The women were instructed, "Now go and give this message, [that Jesus] isn't here! He has come back to life! Give this message to his disciples *including Peter*" (Mark 16:7 TLB; italics added). The Lord did not want Peter to brood any longer about how he'd denied knowing his Master, Messiah, and Friend. Remember how Jesus cared for Peter someday when *you* may feel like Peter! Jesus's archenemy—Satan—will always do everything to have you give in to his various ways of temptation, and secondly, he'll try to convince you that the Lord doesn't want you back—that you're so bad and you've blown it so greatly with God! *Not!* Remember Peter's denial and Jesus's forgiving and welcoming Spirit for Peter.

Something to consider here, as we look to Peter as a type of role model for us, is Jesus said, "Simon, Simon, Satan has asked to have you … but I have pleaded in prayer for you that your faith should not completely fail. So when you have repented and turned to me again, strengthen and build up the faith of your brothers" (Luke 22:31–32 TLB). The apostle Peter was named Simon, only to have Jesus change his name to Peter, meaning "the Rock." We should see and remember that Jesus wanted Peter to develop and grow; his "faith should not completely fail" (Luke 33:31 TLB). Jesus knew that Peter would someday need to have the type of faith that would allow him to further the kingdom here on earth and likewise be able to "strengthen and build up the faith of [his] brothers" (Luke 22:32 TLB).

This is terrific news for us too! When we sin, when we disappoint, maybe even deny our knowing Christ, *it isn't over for us!* No. "So when we have repented and turned to [Jesus] again, [we can pray for Christ to] strengthen and build up [our] faith, so we may work to build up the faith of [our] brothers" (Luke 22:31–32 TLB). Do not allow Satan to fill you with the lies regarding what happens when we fall on our faces in front of our Lord! The Lord's promise in Deuteronomy 31:6 (NIV), "Never leave you nor forsake you" doesn't have an expiration date, nor is it a limited offer coupon deal. No, it's for real; it can't run out, and it goes all the way back to Moses's sending forth the children of Israel before crossing into the Promised Land. Peter, as predicted by Jesus, denied Christ under extreme pressure, and Christ made sure that Peter knew He had risen! Yes, Christ was (and is) alive! Peter was not cast off by Jesus; no, Christ told Peter, "I have pleaded in prayer for you that your faith should not completely fail" (Luke 22:31 TLB). I am sure that Jesus prays so that your (and my) faith should not completely fail either.

Glory to God! We are not forgotten by our Lord Jesus Christ. His words have endured for more than 2,000 years! How *cool* is that?

Reflection: Have you ever denied knowing Jesus? Has there been a time when you rejected Him? Think of how defeated Satan will be from now on when you bow your head and your heart, seek the Lord's forgiveness, and are welcomed back into Jesus's open arms, as Peter was.

LEADERSHIP LESSONS FROM THE APOSTLE PETER

We have already identified Peter as being *fiery*. Additional portrayals of Peter have been *brash, impetuous, impulsive,* and *emotional*. What might be learned about Peter's *leadership abilities*? Peter may have been the most outspoken of the twelve apostles in Jesus's ministry on earth. He was considered a part of the inner circle of Jesus's followers with James and John. Peter certainly became one of the boldest witnesses for the faith. In Matthew 16:16, we learn that Peter was the *first* to call Jesus the Son of the Living God—the Messiah. Perhaps as a type of reward for the answer to Jesus's questions "Who are the people saying I am?" and "Who do *you* think I am?" (Matthew 16:13, 15 TLB), Jesus began Peter's leadership role, not only for the disciples and himself. This would carry Peter out into his activities while growing the church after Jesus's Ascension. Jesus said to Peter, "God has blessed you … for my Father in heaven *has personally revealed this* to you—this is not from any human source" (italics added; Matthew 16:17 TLB).

When Jesus called him, Peter knew that He was of God and felt unworthy to be in Jesus's presence (Luke 5:6–8). Even so, Jesus did not hesitate and told Peter and his brother Andrew that He would make them "fishers of men" (Mark 1:17 NIV).

It might be said that the relationship between Peter and Jesus bonded even further when Jesus called on Peter to meet him *on the lake*, as Christ called Peter to walk with Him *on* the water. Likewise, it could be said that Peter passed an important test of his faith in Jesus, very revealing, to put it mildly. I don't know about you, but I feel that I have "stepped out in faith" in my life, but my experiences can't hold a candle to the *step in faith* talked about in Matthew 14:22–33. What is truly inspiring is that after Jesus called out to the men, it was Peter who replied, "Sir, if it is *really you*, tell me to come over to you, walking on the water" (italics added; Matthew 14:28 TLB).

Friends who have been in the military have told me that the motto is "Don't volunteer for anything." Well, Peter surely did volunteer to meet Christ and walk to Him on the water. Talk about an amazing level of faith! Yes, Peter had great faith!

You could look at Peter also and focus on his shortcomings. There were patterns of behavior that we would not want to emulate. Peter had some prejudices. He had problems giving equal treatment to Gentile Christians. Peter had difficulties with giving up the Jewish traditions. We've previously mentioned that Christ came into the world to do away with the Jewish customs and traditions. Under the covenant that God created for the Israelite people, when He gave the Law to Moses, there were multiple sacrifices—animal sacrifices—necessary for the people to remain in God's good graces. History indicates that the people, although they had so many acts of mercy and grace from God, so many times turned away from God. It took God's sending none other than His very own Son (Jesus) to be sacrificed—the ultimate and final sacrifice—to save those who will acknowledge their sins and come to follow God's Son, Jesus the Christ. When that occurs, the only law necessary is the model given us by Christ Himself.

As far as leadership is concerned, there should be no confusion with respect to Peter's being a front-runner among Jesus's disciples. Jesus spoke of Peter, "I tell you that you are Peter, and on this rock I will build my church, and the gates of Hades will not overcome it" (Matthew 16:18 NIV). What an endorsement, right? I can do nothing but envy Peter's position with regard to his understanding of the role he was expected to play. Peter, *the rock*, was a "go-to person" when Jesus walked this earth, and Peter figured powerfully after Christ's Ascension. My envy is contained in the supervisory relationships I experienced during my non-educator experiences.

Most times, I felt the support of my immediate supervisors. Sadly, through no fault of my own, even though it was the right thing to do as

I made decisions, I did not always have the benefit of strong immediate senior reports. In other words, these managers were usually more political than practical. Pragmatism over personal interests, even when the right thing to do wasn't the most popular and could've attracted a negative impact, was not employed. It might be said that there was little intestinal fortitude employed (if you know what I mean) in some tough decisions.

Back to Peter. In 1 Peter 1:13–16, Peter gives instructions to those pursuing leadership roles. But as an aside, I have found that leadership doesn't always mean you must be out in front. For example, when I was first elected to be a township commissioner, the other board members elected me to be president of the board. What an amazing honor! It was especially humbling, given I was the youngest member of the board—one of the youngest to even be elected a township commissioner in my township! I served in that capacity for six years.

Eventually I was replaced as the president. That didn't prevent my being able to lead. There are times when leadership is fluid. Based on the events of the times, the leadership role may be shared. For the last twenty-five years, I have led causes important to the township residents "from the side," meaning I still made my opinions known and those of my constituency, regardless of my place at the board table.

Peter writes, "Gird up the loins of your mind, be sober … rest your hope fully upon the grace … of Jesus Christ" (1 Peter 1:13 NKJV). Men in Jesus's time would tighten their robes to avoid getting caught on obstacles as they walked. So a good leader remains focused on the tasks at hand, not being easily distracted by other issues. A good softball hitter doesn't take her eye off the ball while at bat. Distractions in that situation will create strikeouts, enough of which will land her on the bench a lot or removed from the team.

"Be sober … rest your hope fully upon the grace … of Jesus Christ" (1 Peter 1:13 NKJV). Being sober doesn't have to always coincide with the use or avoidance of some type of chemical stimulus. I've known people who were drunk or high on other than chemical stimuli. Be there issues with power, popularity, or control, in many ways they were very ineffective as leaders. For years, I have described my leadership style as being driven by humility. I have said, "I really don't think that much of myself." When I have told people this, some have taken the opportunity to stop me and provide me with a mini-lecture, pep talk, or counseling session to point out that I shouldn't put myself down. Hello! I am not putting myself down! I simply wish to avoid becoming what used to be more commonly stated as "puffed up." You know the type—so impressed with themselves that they try to make others feel insignificant or lower than them. I have been a township commissioner for more than three decades—I am comfortable in the role—but I am still a little uncomfortable when constituents or township employees address me as "Commissioner." I know that it's out of respect and appropriate, but I just can't seem to get used to the idea. I am no more important or better than anyone else. I have been elected to serve in a leadership role that affects the livelihood of many people. It is humbling (or *not*, depending on how the individual approaches it!). Unfortunately, some people who, as my dad used to say, "are really full of themselves" look at this role and somehow get "drunk" or "high" on their position. They would do well to exercise Peter's directive "Be sober ... rest your hope fully upon the grace ... of Jesus Christ" (1 Peter 1:13 NKJV). At our public township meetings, the president of the board reads a prayer. For some people, that might be a formality. We have been questioned by some who find this prayer to be inappropriate at a public meeting. The prayer is nondenominational and does not celebrate or revere any particular religion over any others. Even though the same prayer is read at every meeting, I take it seriously—I appreciate the sentiment—and view it as the prayer of its intentions. Of course, I pray for our board in my personal prayer time as well.

Peter goes on to instruct his readers to "rest [their] hope *fully* upon the grace ... of Jesus Christ" (italics added; 1 Peter 1:13 NKJV). We all know folks who have had, and perhaps *we* have had, times in our lives when *hope* has eluded us. I have often thought and shared with others that I can't imagine living without the relationship I have with God. It seems every day you can be inundated with TV commercials and letters in the mail asking for contributions that will fill a need, giving hope to people who may be described as hope*less*. If you think about it, there are even organizations out there seeking funding for animals who "have no hope" and are neglected.

Peter writes, "Rest your hope fully upon the grace ... of Jesus Christ" (1 Peter 1:13 NKJV). Do you see what I see? We've talked about it many times already in this book—*grace!* Our hope should "rest fully upon the grace of Jesus Christ" (1 Peter 1:13 NKJV). So what's the impact here? Sometimes hope is all someone has to count on in their life. When they open their eyes in the morning, what they see around them is so bleak that, without the hope that somehow things will get better that day, they might not want to continue living! You've heard the expression "There but by the grace of God, go I" (John Bradford, circa 1510–1555). Well, that is exactly what Peter is advocating here! "Rest your hope fully upon the grace of Jesus Christ" (1 Peter 1:13 NKJV).

Let's take this a little further. As a leader, sometimes decisions have to be made that will be difficult to take or receive for those being led. So when making the decision, perhaps knowing how the decision will be received, we as leaders need to spread grace over the situation. Sure! The decision is *ours*; I get that! But showing grace to the recipients may make the pill a little easier to swallow. As a leader, you may ask the Lord to grant you the grace to spread upon the others. "Rest your hope fully upon the grace of Jesus Christ" (1 Peter 1:13 NKJV) as the leader. Hope that those being led will be able to accept the decision.

Peter goes on to write, "As obedient children, [do] not conform yourselves to the former lusts, as in your ignorance" (1 Peter 1:14 NKJV). You say, "Thanks, Pete, but that's easier said than done!" Have you ever noticed how easy it seems to be to fall back into your old habits? Interestingly, when I first moved to PA, I wanted to lose my New York City accent. *(What?* New Yorkers *have an accent?)* After fifty-plus years of living in PA, you would think I'd've lost the New Yorkese, right? Well, I have—until, that is, I meet a true New Yorker and start to imitate their speech. It throws me "back to the old neighborhood" again, so testifies my family. Anyway, Peter warns us to safeguard our hearts through our actions. If I am not *right with God* for some reason, it affects everything I do! My attitude is terrible, and I am really not fit to be around. As a leader, making wise decisions will be hampered under these conditions. This is why Peter tells us to "not conform [ourselves] to the former lusts, as in [our] ignorance" (1 Peter 1:14 NKJV). When Christ came into my heart, the Bible says I became reborn! I became a new person! So reverting to my "former lusts, as in [my] ignorance" (1 Peter 1:14 NKJV), will certainly limit my effectiveness for God!

Verses 15 and 16 give us the direction we need to be the effective leaders we all hope for. Peter writes, "As He who called you is holy, you also be holy in all your conduct, because it is written, 'Be holy, for I am holy'" (1 Peter 1:15 NKJV). Peter quoted the words God spoke as recorded in Leviticus 11:44–45 (NIV). As an aside, this is what I love about scripture—its authenticity! How cool is it that Peter quoted what God said through Moses, the dates of these events being circa 1445–1444 BC (and yes, I still say BC and AD; call me old-fashioned, I guess). As leaders, Peter is directing us to the lifestyle modeled by Jesus Christ. Briefly looking over the life of Christ, recall that God sent His Son Jesus into the world not as a conqueror, not as an intergalactic alien, but as a human child—a baby born just as other babies are delivered. Remember except for the inability to sin, Christ experienced everything else a human could have to happen to her or him. We know that Christ became angry and disappointed, He wept over the loss of friends and loved ones, and He showed compassion and pity.

Why bring this all up here? Well, if we're talking about leadership, and we want to look for a model, we can take Jesus's example, and with the help of the Holy Spirit, who has the heart of Christ, we can do it! As Peter directs us, through God's Word as written by Moses in the Leviticus selection, if we take on the mantel of holiness, think of how much different our leadership will be. Think about the leaders you have had—scouting, sports or academic teams, and supervisors at your workplaces. Were any of them of the caliber of "holiness"?

So whether you want to be or currently are a leader, how will you use what we have just discussed together? Will you leave your old self behind, never to return to the lusts that you engaged out of ignorance? Can you entertain the concept of placing your conduct under the influence of the Holy Spirit, whereby you may become holy? Peter referenced the words of God through Moses, that all your conduct must be holy, for as it is written of God, "Be holy, for I am holy" (1 Peter 1:16 NKJV).

Reflection: If you have been in a leadership role, think about your *leadership style*. Are you considering decisions now? I challenge you to consider past decisions and put them through a "holiness test." What will you currently do, and how could past decisions have been improved?

EVERYONE NEEDS A MENTOR

Titus 2:1–8

This section is titled "Everyone Needs a Mentor," and I believe that. To try to make it through life without someone to look up to does not appear in any writing entitled "The Key to Living a Successful Life Is …" *Everyone needs a mentor.* My first real job was as a bank teller. I knew nothing about being a bank teller. I may have mentioned that as I went to work on the first day, my dad said, "Bring home some samples!" Even so, Dad was proud of me. Having his son working at a bank was a big deal for him.

An early mentor in my life was my older cousin Billy. He was the first grandchild on my mother's side of the family. Billy was four years older than me and really smart. But that's not what attracted me to him, as I considered recognizing him as a mentor. Billy was—and is—just a nice guy to be around. His even-temperedness, even as a young boy, places him high on the "I want to be like Billy" scale as far as I'm concerned. Another factor was when Billy and I were sea scouts. Billy joined first, so he was already solidly established when I came into the picture. Ten years old was the official enrollment age, but arrangements were made for me to get in at age eight because my dad was willing to be a volunteer leader. But truth be known, I *really wanted* to be a sea scout. Why? Of course, because Billy was one! Additionally, I just watched how Billy interacted with other people, and he just always gave off the types of signals that endeared others to him. He wasn't flashy; he was honest and reliable—the kind of guy you'd want to be around when the chips were down.

Another mentor was the head teller at the office where I worked. She had been working there for many years by the time I was hired. She was very patient with me. Just to give you an idea of *how patient*, when I received my very first paycheck, I took it to her to have it cashed. However, I was very new to anything having to do with business. When I took her the check, she very politely told me that I had signed the pay stub on the back, not the actual check. Embarrassing? Oh yeah. At that moment, no one would have put any money on the idea that one day I would actually become a vice president of that very same bank! So Candy, the head teller, was my first nonfamilial mentor.

I had another mentor at the bank after I graduated from college. I became an assistant manager. My boss's name was Ron. There was a certain amount of *smooth* to Ron that interested me. He was always professionally dressed, and through that trait, it was impressed upon me that this is how it was expected I would conduct myself—professionally—while working in management with him. Probably the best lesson I learned from Ron was "Be firm but fair when dealing with customers and the personnel who work under your supervision." You know, I believe that statement has followed me the closest throughout my life. As a coach, a baseball umpire, as a parent, as a supervisor, a teacher, and yes, even as a township commissioner, I have practiced the axiom "Be firm, but fair ..."

There was a man I served with, another commissioner named Jack P., who was for me the epitome of *classy*. He was a vice president for the firm where he worked, and he always seemed to see things from the most positive viewpoints possible. For political reasons, Jack declined to be elected to the president's seat, but he encouraged and supported me for the position. Also, Jack was old enough to have been my father, but he always treated me as an equal colleague. Even down to his language, he was one to be copied. I am trying to replicate Jack's style as we currently have a young man on the board. I could be his father, but just as Jack treated me, I am looking at him as my fellow commissioner. I know that I can benefit from listening and learning from my new colleague.

You know, there is a difference between being a *boss* as that compares to being a *supervisor or mentor*. It took me a whole career, but I finally was blessed to have two people as my immediate superiors who never made me feel *inferior*, as they were my superiors by design through the organizational chart. My assistant principal was always trying to make the work environment more attractive and positive. So much so that he actually painted areas in the building following the school colors! I'm not kidding! One day I reported to school and sections of the school were painted bright orange! It was amazing! So Tyler was fortunate enough to be mentored by our mutual superior, Melissa. Where would I start to describe this phenomenal woman to you? This woman just opened herself up to all who would be honest enough to give her a chance to influence their life. She wasn't afraid to share her vulnerability, which gave all those around her the OK to be vulnerable themselves. You see, I think that given the right environment, we have the best chance to grow when we allow ourselves to be vulnerable. Many days, Melissa and Tyler would be outside welcoming students to school—without regard for the weather that day. On the first day of what turned out to be my last year of teaching, Melissa and Tyler "talked me off the ledge" as I was being faced with a teaching situation that I saw as impossible for me to handle. Truth be known, I almost quit on the first day that year. Melissa gave me a hug that, except for my wife, no one else can ever match. She and Tyler pledged their support, and I probably had one of the best years *ever* in the classroom. Melissa for sure was a terrific mentor to me that year. I love those people!

Titus traveled extensively with the apostle Paul. It is written that Paul mentored Titus, as he had done with others of his time. In the above passage, Paul makes clear what the appropriate role is for Titus, for a cross-section of the society they were living among. Titus was a young man and a relatively new believer. Think about it; Paul had an incredible amount of faith in this mentee to place so much faith in his ability to keep together the new, young churches Paul started.

Paul lectures about older men, older women, younger women, and young men. He is fair as he takes careful aim at working to establish the correct behavior among the people of the churches he ministered to. But it wouldn't be bad if even those outside the church were to adopt the behaviors outlined by Paul in the letter to Titus, his mentee.

OK, *older men*, here we go! In verse 2, Paul declares, "Older men [are] to be temperate, worthy of respect, self-controlled, and sound in faith, in love and in endurance" (Titus 2:2 NIV). As an older man, I really feel challenged to emulate this type of behavior. Since I turned seventy, I admit that I have become a bit self-regulating in my thinking. In other words, I am sometimes prone to take on the attitude that now that I'm a senior I rarely need to ask permission to do much of anything. *I won't apologize for my actions!* So as an older man, instead of getting cantankerous, I need to behave more moderately—*temperate*, to be exact. It stands to reason that for me to be *worthy of respect*, self-control would be a requisite. We may as well continue with Paul's Titus letter, which says "sound in faith, in love and in endurance" (Titus 2:2 NIV). Well, older men, this is no small order. No, but I can see the importance of it all. Older men, whether we like it or not, depending on the venue there will always be younger folks around who will be watching to see what we're going to do, given any situation. So *old men*, what are we going to give these youngsters to look at? What will they be able to take with them that's of any value, to be used sometime at a later date in *their* lives? Don't underestimate your position in the room. "Older men ... be temperate, worthy of respect, self-controlled, and sound in faith, in love and in endurance" (Titus 2:2 NIV). Ask God for the ability, and He will give you what you'll need to pull this off.

Think about some of the older men you've known in your lifetime. Why do they stick out in your memory right now? What are the traits that you can recall? Were they respectful? Did they display self-control? Was their faith sound—you know, when the chips were down, when they or their loved ones were facing crises? Did they know what to do or where to turn? And lastly, did they show love and did they give up or stand strong and make you feel like they could be trusted to get through whatever the crisis was? I hope that my family might one day say that as an older man I was able to exemplify the characteristics in the Titus letter. I know that if I do carry out these traits, I can do them *only* with the help of God!

Admittedly, as an older man, I can be and perhaps am randomly tetchy, but I should always be open to how I might find substance in whatever anyone may be able to share to improve my situation in life. I'd learned that I could absolutely learn valuable lessons, even from my teenage students. Lately, I have been blessed to be serving with a younger man I encouraged to run for president of our commissioner board. I have told him this. He has a talent that empowers him to bring the best out in those he serves with and those he gives service to. Dean can typically take a charged event and back down the volume, making it easier and more natural to listen to the viewpoints of the stakeholders, creating win-win situations. I think this is a gift, a talent that not everyone is equipped with. I'm not sure this can necessarily be taught. I expect there are courses out there, but Dean's approach is innate. I am very glad to be able to watch this younger man in action. It's my privilege.

Paul instructs Titus, in verses 6 through 8, "Encourage the young men to be self-controlled … set them an example by doing what is good … show integrity, seriousness and soundness of speech …" (Titus 2:6–8 NIV). My dad was a punster—no doubt about it! Anyone who knew him would confirm that for sure. I have managed to carry on the tradition. Why do I bring this up? "Soundness of speech" might exclude the practice of punning. Certainly, there are those who are very much entertained by good puns, but admittedly, *too much of a good thing can go too far*. I get it. I have really tried to be selective regarding times and places to interject the puns. So for all you "old men" punsters out there, try to limit your punning, leaving your audiences eager to hear more, as opposed to saying, "[Your name], really? Isn't that enough already?"

The rest of verse 8 concludes by giving us another reason for "soundness of speech that cannot be condemned" (Titus 2:6–8 NIV). Paul writes, "So that those who oppose you may be ashamed because they have nothing bad to say about us" (Titus 2:8 NIV). Wow! Could this actually be a remedy to ward off condemnation of what we say? An antidote for criticism from our opponents? We have discussed constructive criticism earlier in this book. So being constructively criticized can be very helpful. But criticism just to pick on others is not OK. Listen to Paul. Encourage the young and set them an example. But how? By doing good! Teach them through high amounts of integrity, be serious when necessary—don't blow it by not knowing when to joke and when to be staid—and be sound of speech. If you do these things, Paul tells us that condemnation from others will be limited. Glory to God!

Reflection: Depending on what phase of life you are in right now, it's safe to say that mentorship should be taking some form for you. As we take a peek into Paul's advice to Titus, we can identify direction for ourselves as well. Take the opportunity to examine your life. Identify people in your life who have mentored you—formally or just as a matter of choice. What value did they add for you? Look for ways to help others, using your successes and tries not realized (failures?) to guide folks along their way.

USE THE RIGHT EQUIPMENT
TO GO INTO BATTLE

Ephesians 6:13–18

The scene shows the apostle Paul imprisoned in Rome, writing to the Christians in Ephesus. This church was established in AD 53 as Paul was headed on his way home to Jerusalem.

Paul writes, "Use every piece of God's armor to resist the enemy wherever he attacks, and when it is all over, you will still be standing up" (Ephesians 6:13 TLB). Paul eventually lays out for us what the pieces of God's armor are. I've heard and read that there are Christians who do not acknowledge the character Satan. Well, I don't like to dwell on Satan, but I certainly know that this evil character is spoken of in scripture. In fact, the Bible tells us that Jesus Himself was tormented and Christ resisted the devil. James 4:7 reads, "So give yourselves humbly to God. Resist the devil and he will flee from you" (James 4:7 TLB). This is terrific advice—good counsel. I have sensed situations where Satan was trying to get into my head—no, sneakier, into my spirit! Here's what I pray: "In the name of Jesus, through the power of the Holy Spirit, 'Get thee behind me, Satan!'" (ref. Matthew 16:23 KJV). *Immediately!* Any remnant of the *feeling* of any evil presence *is gone!* Glory to God!

When Paul writes, "Use every piece of God's armor to resist the enemy wherever he attacks, and when it is all over, you will still be standing up" (Ephesians 6:13 TLB), believe the scriptures here! Christianity is a way of life that takes time to become second nature for you. *Believing* is the first step. *Seeing* and *experiencing His wonders* will come as you give over more and more of your life to the Lord. After my dad became a Christian, he had many questions about this newfound faith. Dad went and spoke with our pastor about his questions. The pastor told him, "Bill, don't worry. Believe as much as you can understand [at the moment]." This allowed my father to grow in his walk with Christ.

If you were a Roman soldier in Paul's day, you would have worn a belt for the tethering of your sword, one of the weapons of choice, which was standard issue. Of course, the steel breastplate was likewise crucial to the protection of the body. So for Paul, the "Belt of truth" (Ephesians 6:14 TLB) lends itself as a metaphor to help us understand how God wants us to live our lives. Think of it—*truth* as a weapon fastened to the body of our personage, our reputation. And then the breastplate is *God's approval*! For us to attain the approval of Almighty God, we need to wield the sword of *truth*!

One day, having the opportunity to speak with a student privately, I shared my chagrin regarding the generation he was a part of. I confessed my concern over the general behavior patterns of his generation. You see, I told him that I have a granddaughter who was his age. All too often, the young people today do not feel the need to be truthful. They will lie profusely and so easily rather than be truthful, even if it means having to face immediately negative circumstances. I was able to recount the story of how my wife and I "shook on" the agreement to buy our home; our "word" was enough for the seller, and his "word" was fine with us. We were all *truthful people!*

Speedy shoes are talked about next. "Wear shoes that are able to speed you on as you preach the Good News of peace with God" (Ephesians 6:15 TLB). Unfortunately, this is probably, believe it or not, the weakest area in my walk with Christ. I'm not necessarily going to ignore my love of God, but there have certainly been times in my life where I could have been bolder for the Lord. Another Bible translation reads, "With your feet fitted with the readiness that comes from the gospel of peace" (Ephesians 6:15 NIV). "Readiness." Maybe this is where I can improve my CE (Christian effectiveness). I need to be ready for anything that God may put in my path for Him and His kingdom. My "readiness" will be improved as I "wear shoes that are able to speed [me] on as [I] preach the Good News of peace with God" (Ephesians 6:15 TLB). Is any of this making sense now that you are this far into the book? This all should be influencing you with the idea that every day is a day to be lived within the power of the Holy Spirit. I've said it before: walking with Christ is a way of life!

Back to the warrior's armor. "In every battle you will need *faith as your shield* to stop the fiery arrows aimed at you by Satan" (Ephesians 6:16 TLB; italics added). Those "fiery arrows" can come from many and diverse directions. Since we don't live in a "perfect world," few of us are immune from the fiery arrows' effects. Usually, the attacks are not foreseeable either.

Let's think about the sources of these *fiery arrows*. Here is a list (not complete, I'm sure): health, wealth, coworkers, superiors, subordinates, neighbors, fellow students, parents, children, siblings, extended family, spouses, acquaintances, or strangers.

Wow! How do we even get out of bed every morning? What can we do to wrap our heads around the very idea that the approximately dozen sources of "fiery arrows" might very well originate from this list? I can't see anywhere or anyone in my life that from whom the "fiery arrows" wouldn't be a potential threat for me.

OK, so to combat the instigators, what does Paul instruct us to do? He says, "Take up the shield of faith [in Christ Jesus as Lord], with which you can extinguish all the 'fiery arrows' of Satan" the Evil One (Ephesians 6:16 TLB; quotation marks added). You see, although we have identified many people, even potentially those close to us personally, we must allow ourselves to believe that because of the Evil One, Satan, even if these people don't represent most of the originators of the fiery arrows, they might be *used by the devil* to get to us. Recall the metaphor of armor: the belt of truth and breastplate of God's approval.

We might attest to the fact that any and all of the originators previously mentioned above could create *issues* for us to deal with. Yes, even our loved ones can disappoint us and potentially alienate us to them at times. Do they necessarily stop loving us? No, I don't think so. They are just *not acting* the way *we wish they would*. They become the shooters of the "fiery arrows" that Paul speaks of.

How are we directed to handle this? Put on the belt of truth, the breastplate of God's approval, wear *speedy shoes*, and "in every battle you will need faith as your shield." Wait! We're not finished! "You will need the helmet of salvation and the sword of the Spirit—which is the Word of God" (Ephesians 6:17 TLB). Can you be a Christian without reading the Bible? Yes! Yes, you can! But you won't grow in the faith. Life doesn't automatically get to be perfect or even all that much easier when you accept Christ as your Savior and Redeemer. I hate to burst your bubble in this one. Becoming a Christian guarantees you an eternal life in heaven. After praying the salvation prayer, what was it I told you to do? You should walk into a church the very next Sunday and begin to worship as a new believer! "How do I find a good church?" you ask. You might ask a churchgoing neighbor or even a coworker if you might go to church with them. The point is you need to begin to wake up to faith—putting your faith into practice as soon as possible. You will begin growing your faith in Christ and developing a relationship with Him. I might add here that you should try to meet with the pastor of the church and seek assistance as you look for a Bible to begin reading daily. This is the subject matter for another book.

Paul concludes his letter with what I consider maybe the most important advice. "Pray all the time. Ask God for anything in line with the Holy Spirit's wishes. Plead with Him, reminding him of your needs" (Ephesians 6:18 TLB). I believe in prayer so much that I've devoted an entire section on it, as you've read.

Will Rogers was known as a cowboy philosopher. He is remembered as having said, "I never met a man I didn't like" (Pinterest.com). I like to say, "I never met-a-phor I didn't like." Jesus and now Paul used parables, simple stories to illustrate moral or spiritual lessons conveyed to get points across to their followers. Taking this form of communication into consideration, you may wish to reread the scripture passage of this section and personalize it to *your life*. I would conclude by saying that life is tough with or without your being a Christian. Knowing, loving, and following Christ and His teachings will help you cope with *whatever* life throws your way.

Reflection: Stop for a moment, and examine the situation you may be facing and dealing with. Take the time to pray. "Ask God for anything in line with the Holy Spirit's wishes. Plead with him, reminding him of your needs" (Ephesians 6:18 TLB). I am going to go out on a limb here and predict that God will show you how to either save you from harm or improve upon what good is going on in your life *right now!*

LOOK FOR THE TRUTHS THAT COME OUT OF AFFLICTION

James 1:2–8 (TLB)

Twenty-five years ago, I was introduced to James 1:2–8. This is another example of the Bible using a metaphor to communicate a point of belief. I have read this passage in several translations. I encourage you to do likewise. The Living Bible paraphrase (not a translation per se) seems to me to be very helpful for a new believer.

James, the author of this book of the Bible, was Jesus's brother and a leader of the church in Jerusalem. Interestingly enough, the letter was written exactly 1,900 years before I was born (in 1949, some more useless trivia). James's audience were first-century Jewish Christians residing in Gentile (non-Jewish) communities outside Palestine and of course all Christians everywhere (including you and me).

So James starts off by asking a somewhat controversial question. "Is your life full of difficulties and temptations?" (James 1:2 TLB). Wow! What a way to start a letter! Do you think James is trying to encourage his readers to get into his letter?

We know that James wrote to Jewish Christians who had been scattered (known as a diaspora) in the areas throughout the Mediterranean Sea. They were scattered because of persecution. As an aside, when I taught about the religions of the world, and as we learned about Christianity, I used to ask my students, "Was Jesus a Christian?" I am sure you can imagine the answer. These were twelve- and thirteen-year-old children. "Yes!" was their response. When I corrected them to tell them that Christ was a Jew, I had a bit of a battle royal on my hands.

Those Jews who accepted Jesus as their personal Savior did not have an easy time of it. Worshiping outside the Jewish traditions too often placed them in physical and social danger. To complicate the matter even more, in those times, there were politics involved as well. The Jewish nation existed within the geographic confines of the Roman Empire. The Jewish leaders who conspired with the Romans to crucify Christ still ruled the everyday lifestyles of the people. Take a moment to imagine what life might have been like in those times.

Thank God my immediate family members are Christians! Glory to God! *But* we are not at all on the same page politically. Can you see where I'm going with this? All Americans should thank Jesus that we live in a country where we can openly worship our God without fear of retribution. As we've described, the Jews were not only ruled by the Roman government of the time, but they were also governed with ordinances within the Jewish religion. The Jewish hierarchy was recognized by the Roman Empire. You might reflect on the trials of Jesus, including how Christ was handed back and forth among the Roman authorities. You'll recall that the Jewish officials wanted Christ killed, but they didn't have the authority to crucify Jesus themselves. The Jewish authorities trumped up charges against Jesus and made them stick before the Roman emperor. With Jesus having been identified by the Jewish religious higher-order authorities as "Public Enemy Number One," Jewish people oftentimes were snubbed and drummed out of their families for professing their belief in Christ as their Savior after His Ascension. This is why religious liberty is so important in America. May we never lose it!

To say these people lived under hostile conditions would be an understatement. We know how Saul of Tarsus (history knows him as Paul, one of the greatest apostles ever known) was commissioned by the Jewish authorities to round up as many Jewish believers in Christ as he could find. It is possible that Saul witnessed the trial of Stephen, who became the first Christian martyr (Acts 7:54–60). We see in Acts 7:58 that Stephen's executioners laid their garments in front of Saul, lending to the idea that Saul had been actively involved and approved of Stephen's death. Saul later devastated the church, entering people's homes and imprisoning the "ringleaders," and Saul's brutal enthusiasm motivated him to lock up female believers as well.

Is your life full of difficulties and temptations? Considering what we know about how *difficult* the living was for those newly converted Jews to Christianity, how could James in good conscience actually write this? Let's be careful that we don't cast a shadow over this question that could make it appear that James was being at all glib as he wrote this.

Is your life full of difficulties and temptations? We have already identified and discussed the *difficulties* here. So what of *temptations?* I am sure that the people of that day struggled with some of the same physical and social issues that we do. Considering the religious hardships they faced, I dare say we probably cannot personally identify with them. The newly converted believers would probably have been hounded to quit believing these *silly notions!* Their nonbeliever families would certainly have been reproaching them by saying, "Your salvation is based on believing that *one day* God will send us our Redeemer, but *this Jesus wasn't the One!*" If the Jewish believers were to reveal themselves on this, they would've been shunned and drummed out of the family and perhaps even out of the community. So this was no small *inconvenience;* this represented a major life change.

Don't be misled here. *Is your life full of difficulties and temptations?* I am sure there are some of my readers who can relate to the statement "Are you kidding me? What's with this newfound religion all of a sudden? Why are you hanging around that church all the time lately?" I get it. I am grateful that my family members are all in with Christ. If your life is full of difficulties and temptations, James provides you with a remedy, as he did for those scattered Jewish Christians in AD 49.

"Be happy, for when the way is rough, your patience has a chance to grow. So let it grow, and don't try to squirm out of your problems. For when your patience is finally in full bloom, then you will be ready for anything, strong in character, full and complete" (James 1:2–4 TLB). Boy, if you have a stomachache, an antacid pill surely sounds like a good cure, right? We might look at James's answer and wonder whether his "pill" represents a quick- or slow-acting formula. It will take a certain degree of personal faith in Christ to actually buy into James's answer. "Be happy ..."

Expecting that we will probably *never face* the persecution that those first-century Christians did, perhaps we have a better chance of mustering the "Be happy ..." remedy offered up by James. Nevertheless, James wrote this in his letter.

Where does James go from there? James says, "When the way is rough, your patience has a chance to grow" (James 1:2 TLB). I'm finding out that the older I get, the stronger my patience is than it has been in the past in certain situations and with some people. My family might share that as I've grown older, I have become cantankerous in certain circumstances (and I would tend to agree), but overall, I feel myself being more patient. My wife will attest that I don't honk my horn at red-to-green lights as often as I used to (and that's saying something, having my New Yorker dad drive when I was growing up)!

Time for another metaphor or analogy! You're out and about driving your car. Consider the ease of your drive given different roadway conditions. First, it's a beautiful Sunday afternoon on a superhighway, no traffic at all, with perfect weather conditions! "Rick," you say, "cut me a break! Please don't insult my intelligence. *Of course* I would choose this option!" OK, the next option is driving in a big city during rush hour, and oh by the way, it's raining cats and dogs! Without my giving you the opportunity to interject, lastly, you are driving off-road in your four-wheel-drive Jeep over rocks and crossing small streams.

Considering these options, with which option will you be able to drive more carefree and be able to arrive at a destination more safely and quickly? I think if I were asking James to weigh in, he would say that although the Jeep driving experience would take longer, he would certainly have been forced to develop a greater degree of patience as a result. You see, having to pick his way through the rocks and gingerly crossing the streams, he would need to be more aware of his surroundings and the effects on his vehicle. He may even get to develop a better appreciation for his immediate surroundings as a by-product benefit in the end. "When the way is rough, your patience has a chance to grow" (James 1:2 TLB).

"So let it grow, and don't try to squirm out of your problems. For when your patience is finally in full bloom, then you will be ready for anything, strong in character, full and complete" (James 1:4 TLB). One of the mistaken ideas that people have sometimes been left to believe is that when you ask Christ into your heart, all your problems will be eliminated. You'll never have to face life's problems again. *Not!* No, you aren't *exempted* from life's problems and circumstances; you will be provided *help to live through* them!

James goes on to counsel his audience as to where they can go for help and how they may grow in wisdom as they endure the consequences of their times. Keep in mind that what James said next was a major paradigm shift, regarding what these Jewish believers had ever been taught about their relationship with God. Access to God was in no way *direct* for the average nonclerical Jew.

The Jewish belief was that God lived in the inner sanctum of the temple, in the Holy of Holies. God was not *directly* accessible to the common Jew. At one time in Jewish history, the high priest held the holiest religious position. The priest's role was initiated from Aaron. This practice ceased when the second temple was destroyed. The role of the high priest was to oversee the temple service and act as spiritual leader to the Jewish congregations. The most visible responsibility of the high priest was to enter the Holy of Holies, the area of the temple that was certainly off-limits to the everyday Jew. The high priest entered the Holy of Holies at the most sacred time celebrated by the Jews: Yom Kippur.

"If you want to know what God wants you to do, ask him, and he will gladly tell you" (James 1:5 TLB). Unheard of! *"Ask God?"* You've got to be kidding! Think of the history. Moses saw and spoke with God on Mt. Sinai, and when he came down from the mountain, he had to keep his face covered since it glowed from the experience of being with God. The Jews were taught that God was not spoken to directly. Here comes Jesus's brother, James, who tells these new Messianic Jews (Jews who acknowledged Jesus as the Messiah, their Savior) to just *"ask God."*

James continued. "[God] will gladly tell you [the answers to your questions], for he is always ready to give a bountiful supply of wisdom to all who ask him; he will not resent it" (James 1:5 TLB). For these scattered and oppressed new Jewish believers, this concept would have truly blown their minds! At no time would the rabbinical leaders have ever relinquished their positions of exclusive access to the One True God to anyone, much less the everyday Jew. To have accepted Jesus's free gift of salvation, as a Jew, was much more complicated and difficult than what I did as a sixteen-year-old (Gentile) boy. I was given the invitation, and I simply said yes to Jesus. Finished! I began my Jesus relationship right from there. It was an unintimidated individual decision.

To think of God as *a person* and not just *a deity* would also have been a stretch for these new Jewish followers of Christ. And also take into account that Jesus had been crucified as a criminal! There was danger in the believing for them. I'm not sure I would have been brave enough to declare my belief in Christ under those conditions.

All right, let's relax here a little. We are here in the twenty-first century. We know, James tells us, that "[God] is always ready to give a bountiful supply of wisdom to all who ask him" (James 1:5 TLB). That should provide comfort and serve as a major *tool* for living, if you will. You've been reading about how God's Word has been a type of roadmap over my life, and God can speak to you as well, in many ways, not the least of which is through the scriptures.

Now James seems to really drill down and get focused.

> But when you ask him, be sure you really expect him to tell you, for a doubtful mind will be as unsettled as a wave of the sea that is driven and tossed by the wind; and every decision you then make will be uncertain, as you turn this way, and then that. If you don't ask with faith, don't expect the Lord to give you any solid answer. (James 1:6–8 TLB)

As I have grown in my faith and have been more serious about truly living through commitment to study and prayer, I have been able to see and personally witness results from the power of God. My wife and I have begun to see God at work in our lives more and more all the time.

So many "Godincidences"—not coincidences—have been happening for us. I've previously written a bit about this, but it doesn't hurt to repeat. When you give your very life over to God, He will take it and truly lead you to where He wants to use you. He'll take good care of you as well.

But be sure that when you ask God for something you need (I don't mean a brand-new Rolls-Royce!), please do *your part*. Believe through faith! James writes very pointedly,

> When you ask him, *be sure you really expect him to tell you*, for a doubtful mind will be as unsettled as a wave of the sea that is driven and tossed by the wind; and every decision you then make will be uncertain, as you turn this way, and then that.

> If you don't ask with faith, don't expect the Lord to give you
> any solid answer. (James 1:6–8 TLB; italics added)

I can attest that it takes courage to step out with Christ early in your relationship. As you begin to trust Jesus, your ability to trust Him gets easier, *but* you have to take that first *faith step* that only *you can do* for yourself. So many times in my life, after I'd gotten comfortable with Christ, things were happening, and we seemed unable to handle situations, so I just automatically started praying. God does not turn a deaf ear to us when we ask and believe He will come through for us. Sometimes God responds right away, and other times, He says, "Wait." My point here is that none of this can happen, as I understand James, unless *we believe it can or will happen* as answers from God. "If you don't ask in faith, don't expect the Lord to give you any solid answer" (James 1:8 TLB).

We've covered a lot of ground in this section. It almost reads like a "good news, bad news" type of condition. What I have really tried to project here is that I hear James telling us that the greatest way of life we could ever live is the life of a follower of Jesus Christ! But it won't necessarily be an easy life. When we say yes to Christ, He doesn't tell us that our road will be all downhill. There will certainly be a fair share of uphill struggles, but Christ will be there with and for us, helping us make the climbs.

Are there any math majors in the readership? Try to process this equation:

$$\text{Faith} + \text{Trials} = \text{Patience}$$

Reflection: When was the last time you instinctively looked *upward* to find the wisdom you needed to make a decision about something big in your life? When was the last time you simply misplaced something (maybe something valuable or just needed to have at the time) and *went directly* to the Lord for help to find it? Please take a personal inventory on this, and subscribe to a new paradigm. *Be needy before the Lord*. He wants to be involved in *everything* that you will give Him influence into. Be blessed by the *everyday stuff* that Christ wants to share with you. Be blessed as you venture out in faith with our Lord, and let Him lead during the dance.

PRAISE THE LORD NO MATTER WHAT HAPPENS

Psalm 34:1–11

We are told that Psalm 34 was written by David during a time when he was being hunted by the king of Israel, Saul. In order to throw his hunters off the track, David went to Achish, king of Gath, where he pretended to be insane. In 1 Samuel 21:10–15, we read that David is recognized by the servants of Achish. David became afraid at this point and pretended to be insane. The king scolded his servants, basically saying, "Don't I have enough problems on my hands? Now you think you need to bring me this contemptable guy?" David then escapes.

It is probably safe to assume that everyone has experienced fear at some time in their lives. The scripture passage we are referencing was prompted by David's fear as Saul, the first king of Israel, plotted to kill David because God had anointed David to be Saul's successor to the throne. Maybe we can give Saul a little slack here.

David acknowledges how God responded to his calls. We can be assured that God always hears the cries of those who love Him.

My dear father-in-law, as he is called on to help with some physical chore, is fond of saying, "So what's our plan?" Since no one can predict the future, there is no way to have a formal action plan in place for all possible circumstances in life. Given this reality, David's decision is in verse 1. "I will praise the Lord no matter what happens … I will constantly speak of his glories and grace" (Psalm 34:1 TLB). This is at least a good thought for us to embrace, in lieu of another type of *plan*.

How difficult will it be to emulate David's *plan* for *our* lives? OK, David, you want us to praise the Lord when we get a flat tire on the highway, in the middle of a torrential rainstorm. You want us to praise the Lord when the engine burns up, because the guys at the shop didn't tighten a screw and the oil ran out of the engine. You expect us to praise the Lord when we experience the death of a loved one in our family. Not only is David saying he will praise the Lord, but he finishes by adding, "I will constantly speak of his glories and grace" (Psalm 34:1 TLB). The New International Version translation reads, "His praise will always be on my lips" (Psalm 34:1 NIV) Praise being *always on my lips* makes me feel hopeful as I try to anticipate those times when my heart might be broken, due to the things that can go very wrong in life. I must confess that I haven't always been able to pull this off, and *I won't be able to do this on my own!* Here is where our Lord God will come through for us.

"I will boast of all his kindness to me. Let all who are discouraged take heart" (Psalm 34:2 TLB). The Lord's kindness cannot be overstated. It has always been a mystery to me as to how God can take me, the miserable wretch that I am, and *be kind to me!* What a model for us to try to copy. David must have thought long and hard as he wrote this verse. If you become discouraged, and I am sure he did often during the time frame of when he wrote this psalm, don't! Do not allow discouragement to define you. Lean into the kindness that God offers us. Let "His praise always be on [your] lips." I can attest to this. It's difficult to be cursing and praising the Lord simultaneously. It's *impossible!*

Just think. It seems that David was looking ahead as he wrote these verses. "Let us praise the Lord together, and exalt his name" (Psalm 34:3 TLB). I know my wife and I seem to be praising the Lord at so many turns in our lives. It is much more natural to be praising Him during positive times, but David doesn't limit his praise, does he? Just a reminder, "I will praise the Lord no matter what happens" (Psalm 34:1 TLB) puts the responsibility on us to be praising the Lord *at all times!* I might suggest here that you reach out to at least one other believer who you can share your walk with. You know, a best friend, a spouse, or a sibling who "gets you," someone who will listen more than talk, someone who you can grow with, who will partner with you, so you can "praise the Lord together, and exalt his name" (Psalm 34:3 TLB). It's so great to have a support person, especially as you begin your new life with Christ.

In Psalm 34:4, David explains his reaching out to God and how God answered him. "He freed me from all my fears" (Psalm 34:4 TLB), David states. Can we relate to this in our lives? You know, the fears in life may take on many different forms. We might fear heights (I can relate to that!), we might be afraid of dogs, and loud noises like fireworks displays might drive us indoors with earplugs, not being interested in seeing the beautiful colors in the display. (This is something that bothers my granddaughter.) The loss of employment certainly is fearsome. There are those who fear death—their own or the loss of family members. David explains that God freed him "from all [his] fears" (Psalm 34:4 TLB). Wow! Wouldn't it be a relief if we could cry out to God, explain what we are fearing, and have God *free us from all our fears*? This sounds like something that, in all honesty, would take some time in doing. But here's where our faith comes into play. It'll take some time. But I am ready and willing to start right away! List your fears, take them to the Lord, and let Him free you of them all!

David recognizes that we aren't alone in our quest to live a fear-free life. "Others too were radiant at what he did for them. Theirs was no downcast look of rejection" (Psalm 34:5 TLB). The age-old adage, "Misery loves company" (from the play *Doctor Faustus* by Christopher Marlowe) comes to mind here. I see this as David encouraging the sharing of our lives with others who need the Lord as much as we do, and our practicing following-the-Savior-together with them. We might be able to witness an outcome from David writing, "Theirs was no downcast look of rejection." The NIV translation reads, "Those who look at him are radiant, their faces are never covered with shame." That thought is freeing in itself! Looking to God to free us from our fears is not cause for hiding our faces in shame. As we recall that Jesus came to earth as a human being, so He would be able to relate to all the human reactions and feelings that we have. Jesus cares about us! David was moved to write this psalm many years before Jesus was born and walked this earth.

"This poor man cried to the Lord—and the Lord heard him and saved him out of his troubles. For the Angel of the Lord guards and rescues all who reverence him" (Psalm 34:6–7 TLB). There have been lots of times when the Lord saw me in trouble and saved me. I've shared my career twists, where due to political and financial turns I was out of work. Make no mistake. The Lord saved my family and me out of those troubles. When it was discovered that I had three blocked arteries, through my "listening to my body," going to be tested, I was saved from what would have been a major health issue (I might not have survived it), and God saved me out of my trouble. David is giving us permission to cry out to God, and he is telling us that God will be there for us! David also assures us, "The Angel of the Lord guards and rescues all who reverence him" (Psalm 34:7 TLB). I've said it before. This is a personal thing between God and "all who reverence him." It's real!

Somehow, I have never felt comfortable considering *testing God*. But David encourages us to "put God to the test and see how kind he is. See for yourself the way his mercies shower down on all who trust in him" (Psalm 34:8 TLB). As a former educator, *rubric* is a key vocabulary term in the profession. Teachers use rubrics in order to objectively evaluate the correctness, typically to promote the consistent application of learning expectations, learning objectives, or learning standards in the classroom, or to measure their completion against a consistent set of criteria. We might look at what David has directed us to do as we "put God to the test." So as we think about testing God, we do so for very specific reasons, right? "Put God to the test and see how kind he is. See for yourself the way his mercies shower down on all who trust in him" (Psalm 34:8 TLB). We are encouraged to see how kind God is and see for ourselves the way God's mercies shower down on us, if we trust in Him. So you see, we have distinct expectations, objectives, standards, and a way to measure what will happen because of our trust in our great God! Glory to God!

Question: What do you think you would have to do to guarantee your having everything you need? Surely you knew that I would tell you, right? "If you belong to the Lord, reverence him; for everyone who does this has everything he needs ... Those of us who reverence the Lord will never lack any good thing" (Psalm 34:9–10 TLB). What more could any of us wish for?

I've lived long enough to have seen the quality of life of the various classes of people in America. I have seen poor people who were just as happy and contented as anyone could imagine them to be, and I have seen rich individuals who were miserable beyond description. And then there are those who fit somewhere in between.

What would you imagine the causes of the two extremes that I've just described to be? I guess a lot has to do with where a person's value system lies. I don't think that things (toys for grownups too!) necessarily guarantee a happy life. Surely, conveniences are wonderful, but it's interesting to watch the Discovery Channel and see how many more people these days are looking to live off the grid because it's a simpler life. And they're happy! David tells us that if we "belong to the Lord, [and] reverence him, [we] will never lack any good thing" (Psalm 34:9 TLB). You see, it's the good things that I pray my family and I will be blessed with. I am not convinced that all the extras, though convenient, will necessarily be the best for us. As my wife and I raised our two daughters, my wife had a wish to be home with the children. (Lee Ann recalled how nice it was to have her mother there when she got home from school each day, so she could tell her how her day at school went.) We were a single-income household. We can honestly say that we never lacked any good thing.

If we keep the Lord in our sights, following closely behind Him, I interpret David to be telling us that we should be able to live a wonderful life. Here's the synopsis: Be praising the Lord no matter what happens, be constantly speaking of His glories and grace, boast as to the kindness He is showing us, and be praising God and exalting Him with others. Doing these things will place us in the position to cry out to the Lord, expecting He will answer us and free us from all our fears. "The Angel of the Lord guards and rescues all who reverence him" (Psalm 34:7 TLB). Praise and glory be to God.

Reflection: Why not take the time to list your fears and take them to the Lord? Let Him free you of them all! Give these things up to God. Be blessed!

HAVE PATIENCE: GOOD WILL TRIUMPH OVER EVIL!

James 5:1–11 (TLB)

Many years ago, I documented these verses in James. This is another example of the Bible passage having meant so much to me so long ago. I have read this passage in several translations. I encourage you to do likewise. Please allow me to reiterate that The Living Bible paraphrase (not a translation) can be very beneficial for a new Christian.

Just to refresh our memory, James was Jesus's brother and a leader of the church in Jerusalem. James's listeners were first-century Jewish Christians residing in Gentile (another name for a non-Jew) communities outside Palestine.

James begins chapter 5 with a warning. "Now look here" (James 5:1 TLB). "Now listen (James 5:1 NIV). We have noticed in reading James's letter that he relishes the idea of getting his audience to sit up and take notice, even before they know what he's going to say! A sharply toned opening is a surefire way to begin a message. As a teacher, I often used the same tactic or technique. In that sense, it's good to early on get students trying to figure out where the lesson is going.

This is a letter that could easily be misunderstood, but it's an important guideline for sure. "Now listen, you rich people ... your wealth has rotted, and moths have eaten your clothes" (James 5:1–2 NIV). Now depending on your age, you may or may not be able to identify with moth-eaten clothing. My Nana Altes's clothes very often smelled badly, but the stink wasn't body odor! Because she wanted to protect her garments from being eaten by moths, she hung containers, cylinders of camphor balls, in them. You see, moths are not only drawn to flames, but they also love to literally eat clothing made of furs and wool. I dare say that I haven't heard of people using camphor in years! Doing a quick Google inquiry, I read that modern-day prevention involves storing clothes in sealed plastic or other types of garment bags.

If a person has worked hard to accumulate wealth, having to consider that wealth as being subjected to rotting would be very troubling at the least. Wealthy individuals typically adorn themselves with attractive clothing, as well. So here is James asking these rich folks to look at the idea of *rotting wealth and (otherwise) moth-eaten clothes.* Not a pretty picture!

James continued. "Your gold and silver are corroded … you have hoarded wealth" (James 5:3 NIV). See the emphasis on wealth. As a former banker, I certainly have appreciated knowing and working with people who had been able and fortunate enough to have worked, scrimped, and saved money to build monetary security. Most individuals who have wealth have honestly accumulated it. We say these things, while acknowledging the scripture. "For the love of money is a root of all kinds of evil. Some people, eager for money, have wandered from the faith and pierced themselves with many griefs" (1 Timothy 6:10 NIV).

Let's be clear here. Timothy is not condemning or otherwise finding fault with individuals who have accumulated wealth. As an aside, as a young person, I early on had decided that I wanted to go into a profession where people didn't make a lot of money. Do you know *why?* It was because I had misinterpreted 1 Timothy 6:10 to read, "Money is the root of all evil." What a mammoth mistake to have made! Money isn't the root of all evil. *The love of money* "is a root of all kinds of evil" (1 Timothy 6:10 NIV). That is a significant distinction, isn't it? The funny thing is that fifty-plus years ago when I was making those decisions, teachers really were grossly underpaid. Teachers today aren't getting rich teaching, but the remuneration certainly is more reasonably compensating in the current marketplace. Timothy paints with a finer brush here. He writes, "Some people, eager for money, have wandered from the faith and pierced themselves with many griefs" (1 Timothy 6:10 NIV). I have read where persons have worked so very hard to build businesses, they have striven to "climb the corporate ladder," and when they reach their goals, it's all a very shallow existence. When they "have wandered from the faith and pierced themselves with many griefs" (1 Timothy 6:10 NIV), it turns out that they have missed many wonderful things that different choices would have afforded them. Sometimes they have lost otherwise successful marriages, due to neglect they may have had a child get into trouble, and they may have become addicted themselves because of what the job duties required. I am aware of a pastor who said that while standing by the bedside of dying parishioners, none of them in their last breath ever said, "Oh, how I wish I had put more hours in at the office."

So what was James saying in verse 3? Oftentimes, wealthy people are also people in business who are entrepreneurs or at least in positions of authority; thus, they have power over others. James writes,

> The wages you failed to pay the workmen who mowed your fields are crying out against you. The cries of the harvesters have reached the ears of the Lord Almighty. You have lived ... in luxury and self-indulgence. (James 5:3–4 NIV)

I'm sure you are beginning to see James's message here. James is trying to hold those who are the most fortunate—the wealthy—up to a higher standard than others are attaining. In the culture that James lived within, the division between the wealthy and the poor was like a chasm, more than a simple division, such as what the citizens in the US are experiencing. Not only were the well-to-do rich, but there was also little structure in place to care for the common welfare of workers and the poor at large.

I mention this because I'm continuing to strive for our understanding of scripture so that it can speak and be relevant to us in our modern-day environment. Even though we truly can't relate to the life of the listeners of James, Christians can become more aware of those around us who can be helped by us. I've heard it said that even the "poor" in America are much better off than many individuals in some of the world's other countries.

Although we have taken a little detour from the subtitle to this section, "Have Patience: Good *Will Triumph* over Evil!" we did address the first few lines of the identified scripture to do it. James calls upon us to "be patient ... until the Lord's coming" (James 5:7 NIV). Depending upon what is going on in my life, I can be prone to ask Jesus to return to earth and take all His followers and me away with Him to heaven. I don't care whether we are discussing the economy, the political scene, crime in the streets, or a disagreement with a neighbor or relative about any or all of them. Usually, we have little if any direct control over any potential solutions. I think we could agree that all too often the events of our communities and/or the world display evil getting the best of good. When I was a boy, it was said that you could always distinguish the good cowboy from the villain because the good guy wore a white hat. (Roy Rogers—aka a "good guy"—never even had his white hat come off during a fist fight!) If we're not careful, if we don't keep things in perspective, if we don't pray for God's help and understanding, we quite easily can start believing that "good guys finish last," which is another unfortunate saying that I've heard over the years.

But no! James instructs us, "Be patient … until the Lord's coming" (James 5:7 NIV). The joy of following Jesus is that through His sacrifice on the cross for our sins, we have a greater anticipation of the ultimate events of our lives! This world, as we have written before, is not "all there is." Christ will return to earth to take His followers with Him into heaven, to share eternity with Him and His Father—God. That is a promise!

Just in case we can't relate to what being patient looks like, James continued. "See how the farmer waits for the land to yield its valuable crop and how patient he is for the autumn and spring rains" (James 5:7 NIV). My wife's father and mother grew up on farms. They could best relate to the example cited here by James. Maybe those of us from the city, or at least from the suburbs, need to use other indicators for us to relate to the James instruction. Maybe it could read, "See how the baseball fan waits for the weather to yield its warmer temperature and how patient he is for the spring training to begin." Now does that speak to you perhaps a little more closely as a nonfarmer? It takes patience to wait for this every year, doesn't it?

Jesus's disciples suffered much after His Ascension. Almost all of the original twelve died horrific deaths. They lived each day to share the Good News of Jesus! James writes, "Be patient and stand firm, because the Lord's coming is near" (James 5:8 NIV). I'm sure that approximately 2,170 years ago, when James penned this book, he felt Christ's return to be *near.* There are certainly times when based on the events going on around me, and how close to Christ I feel at the time, *I feel Jesus's coming is near.* What does James tell us? "Be patient and stand firm" (James 5:8 NIV). Easier said than done? Yup. But this is where our faith and trust in God becomes so crucial. *Being in Step with God* is the way we are able to carry out the directives from James; we cannot pull this off through our own natural power. We need the supernatural leadership and power of Christ's Holy Spirit.

James seems very uneasy about whether or not we will be able to make this happen. He is so concerned that he cites *examples of patient people* for us. "As an example of patience in the face of suffering, take the prophets who spoke in the name of the Lord" (James 5:10 NIV). Too often the rulers of their times would seek advice and/or predictions, or without their requests the prophets would be called upon by God to go and tell a pharaoh or king what God wanted to have proclaimed, only to have the message not be good for the ruler. In those cases, the messenger would take the brunt of the ruler's wrath. Have you ever heard the saying "I'm just the messenger; don't kill the messenger" when perhaps an employee needed to give news to an owner or supervisor? The point? If we can look to Christ, look to the prophets of old, we have role models to help us remain patient—no matter what is happening around us!

OK, is there any silver lining that might come along with the message from James with regard to patience? James writes, "As you know, we consider blessed those who have persevered" (James 5:11 NIV). Then he goes on to name a real "Olympian" as far as I am concerned! James talks about the Old Testament character Job, who lost everything because of a challenge that God took with Satan. Because he wouldn't turn his back on his God, Job was reduced to a measly form, his home life (he lost almost his entire family to death), his wealth (material possessions), and his health. Nevertheless, Job did what James directs us. "Be patient and stand firm" (James 5:8 NIV). That is exactly how Job handled his situation. (I recommend you read the book of Job, found directly before the psalms.)

"So Schin," you say, "what's the bottom line here?"

"The Lord is full of compassion and mercy" (James 5:11 NIV). I have told people this. "All I know is that I serve a good God, who has my best interests at heart." I cannot explain all that happens to others nor myself;

I just know that God loves me no matter what happens! I believe that Job had the same belief. It was Job's loyalty to his God that brought him through all that Satan did to him indirectly and directly.

"Be patient and stand firm" (James 5:8 NIV). Based on what we have just explored, can you see yourself doing this?

Reflection: How would you paint or describe yourself when it comes to *being patient?* Do you get antsy or restless while waiting for life to take form? At a red light, are you like the drivers in New York City where they blow the horn *even before* the light turns green? Or when the light changes, do you calmly accelerate through the intersection? Well, James tells us, "Be patient and stand firm" (James 5:8 NIV). It is up to us, along with the power of the Holy Spirit, to make that a reality for ourselves.

GROWING IN THE LORD

Ephesians 3:14–21

So what does it take to grow my faith in the Lord? Good question!

The answers may be found in Ephesians 3:14–20. Verse 14 speaks of wisdom. Hmmm. *Wisdom*. The definition of wisdom is the "quality of having experience, knowledge, and good judgment; the quality of being wise; the soundness of an action or decision with regard to the application of experience, knowledge, and good judgment" (Google.com/searchwisdom). The apostle Paul writes,

> When I think of the wisdom and scope of [God's] plan,
> I fall down on my knees and pray to the father of all the
> great family of God—some of them already in heaven and
> some down here on earth—that out of [God's] glorious,
> unlimited resources [God] will give you the mighty inner
> strengthening of his Holy Spirit" (Ephesians 3:14–16 TLB)

"The quality of having experience, knowledge, and good judgment; the quality of being wise" (Google.com/searchwisdom). I've heard, "The only way to get experience at something is *to do* that something." I can attest to the correctness of that saying. My first job at age twenty was working as a bank teller. As I was going to work on my first day, being true to his amazing sense of humor, Dad said, "Bring home some samples!" What a card, right? I had two weeks of training, a few of the most boring days reading and taking short quizzes regarding banking practices. A funny side story: To prepare me, the bank seated me in a very small, enclosed area typically used by customers to review their safe deposit box belongings privately. For about a week, I was cooped up in this tiny booth, to read and get familiarized prior to the actual teller training. I would sit there studying, but from time to time, the activities in the bank branch office sounded unsafe. Only being able to hear without seeing was at times disturbing. I recall one day when the goings-on sounded like the bank was being robbed! Not knowing how to react, I stayed in my booth space. Needless to say, I survived; the bank wasn't held up. Guaranteed, the first day actually on the job was terrifying! I really had no experience as a bank teller. Truth be known, even though I had been given a week's on-the-job-training, on the first day of actually working on my own, my mind went blank and I needed to call my supervisor for her help. Two and a half years later, I was highly respected in that teller role. I was so well-respected that when I graduated from college, I was offered a job as a management trainee. Actually, about twenty years and several other roles later, I became a vice president of that very same bank—a long way away from the teller position. "Who woulda thunk it?"

I might infer that the experiences I'd had were enough to get me the status that I needed to accelerate my career. And it's equally satisfactory to state that I had gained and developed wisdom as well. When it came to dealing with certain banking, business, and other similar focus areas, I was a proficient person to obtain information from. To a certain degree, I was an "expert." There was a degree of wisdom I'd gained as a result.

"Inner strengthening of his Holy Spirit" (Ephesians 3:16 TLB). What does it take to grow your faith in the Lord? Paul directs us to "fall down on [our] knees and pray to the Father … that out of His glorious, unlimited resources He will give you the mighty inner strengthening of His Holy Spirit" (Ephesians 3:14–16 TLB). We never know where and when life's events will touch us.

My wife and I were so thrilled when we became parents for the first time. Our family and friends were excited for us and helped us as the grand event approached. But when the day actually arrived, it was very evident that we were not prepared! We managed to make it through the process. About two and a half years later, it happened again! It's safe to say that we were better prepared the second time. Life gets complicated. Here is where God becomes so very important.

Our walk with the Lord is something that needs to be improved upon as we give the Holy Spirit the opportunity to work in our lives. I'm sure we've all been a trainee at some time in our lives. You know the drill. You wear a name tag that reads, "Rick Schin, Trainee." Your employer wants the customers to know that *you're new*, so that you may be given some leeway as you wait on them. Look out! What comes to mind for me is that familiar five-letter word *grace*. It's an opportunity for the customers to show the trainee grace, overlooking anything awkward or untimely.

We might stretch the point here and say that when someone accepts Christ's free gift, she might be considered a "Christian trainee." The gift of salvation cannot be earned! It's free! But as new Christians, we need to reach out to Christ and let Him and the Holy Spirit work in our lives. As we look to the Lord for His answers and other input, the more we "let go and let God," the better, wiser, and fuller our lives will be developed into. God is "a selfish God"; He wants to have *all of us*. God doesn't want us to be following any other master except Christ. God wishes us to be all in with Him. If you would, recall Ephesians 3:17 (NIV). "And I pray that Christ will be more and more at home in your hearts, living within you as you trust him. May your roots go down deep into the soil of God's marvelous love." God *is* marvelous! When we allow God, Jesus, and the Holy Spirit to have control over our lives, nothing is too big or complicated for the Trinity.

Let us reflect upon the end of verse 17 and consider "God's *marvelous* love" (Ephesians 3:17 TLB; italics added). Ephesians 3:18 (TLB) is so really encouraging to me. "May you be able to feel and understand, as all God's children should, how long, how wide, how deep, and how high his love really is." There are several references that strike me here. My father-in-law was a builder—a carpenter by trade. In his preparations prior to starting a job, Lee would have reviewed an architect's and/or an engineer's plan as to what the construction would require. As I was courting my future wife, at times when I would go to her home, I watched Lee studying plans for a construction job he was either involved in or was soon to be so. He was reading the plans and envisioning what the finished product would look like. He was contemplating *how long, how wide, how deep, and how high* the project was going to be. I am reminded here that Jesus was a carpenter by trade too! This scripture explains that God's "marvelous love" is something that is dimensional in a sense. It's something that we can identify with, see, and hold onto!

"[You will] experience this love for yourselves" (Ephesians 3:19 TLB). God's love will grip us, affect us, and at times overwhelm us if we allow it—no, if we allow *Him*—into our lives! Everyone needs to be loved. "It is so great that *you will never see the end of it* or fully know or understand it" (italics added; Ephesians 3:19 TLB). When we sell out to Christ, when we permit the Holy Spirit to inhabit our spirit, God's love will be evident and a reality for us at all times! Stop! Just take it in. Imagine *real love* twenty-four/seven in your life.

A *love reality* all the time.

Then we read further about the impact of this God connection. "At last you will be filled with God himself" (Ephesians 3:19 TLB). I've shared with you that much of my Christian walk is taken by faith, right? Here is an example of what and how I stand believing. I cannot explain how we are *filled with God Himself*. Briefly, Christianity is based on a supernatural understanding—something I earlier referred to as the Trinity. God, Jesus Christ, and the Holy Spirit represent the deity—that *being, the Person* we can go to for all the answers to the questions and circumstances of life.

God is the One who created the heaven and earth that are written about in Genesis, the first book of the Holy Bible. Jesus Christ came to earth as a human baby, walked the earth, and is written about in the New Testament of the Holy Bible. Christ had a three-year ministry on earth but was put to death—crucified at age thirty-three. Jesus was raised from the dead, and He ascended to heaven. As an important aside, all about Christ was prophesied in the Old Testament. Written in the Holy Bible is the coming of the Holy Spirit. This is written about in Acts 2—in the New Testament. This is called *Pentecost.* When we accept Jesus into our heart, we are essentially bringing the *Holy Spirit* into *fellowship* with *our spirit.* That's a beautiful thing. It's an eternal, redeeming, merciful, gracious act. We have been discussing this throughout the book.

The only thing remaining to say, as we consider our growing in the Lord, is this: "Now glory to God who by his mighty power at work within us is able to do far more than we would ever dare to ask or even dream of—infinitely beyond our highest prayers, desires, thoughts or hopes" (Ephesians 3:20 TLB). This is no small, insignificant statement. Can you see this? This no small, insignificant statement explains the limitless impact that God can have over our lives, if we allow it! The Bible tells us that God's mighty power can be at work within us, to a degree beyond what we could *ever dare to ask or even dream of—infinitely beyond our highest prayers, desires, thoughts, or hopes.* This is available to us if and when we should ask God to bless us with it. Glory and praise to our God!

God wants to dwell in our hearts through the Person of the Holy Spirit. I don't care who you are, someday if not already, you are going to need God for something in your life. I promise it! Without a doubt, I make that statement. God won't turn His back on you. So if you're the type of person who feels you can handle anything and everything that might come down the pike, all by yourself, *that's fine!* I just want to say that there have been life-altering situations in my life that I couldn't have survived had it not been for the grace and mercy of Almighty God! When you give your heart to Jesus, you are signing on for a lifetime of God-directed activities to be unmatched without His influence in your life. I can hear you asking right now, "So are you saying that all I have to do is accept Christ into my life and everything will go perfectly well?" No, I am not saying that at all. God doesn't necessarily prevent heart-aching, heartbreaking events from occurring. Knowing Jesus personally does not necessarily exempt us from the negative challenges in life, even though I know that the Holy Spirit in my family's travels together has protected me on many occasions. Faith in the Trinity will help you to *endure* the hard times, even if you are not going to be *spared* the experiences. You might recall what we talked about when we discussed the scripture passage in James. At the end of the section, I introduced you to the equation "Faith + Trials = Patience." Trials aren't always avoidable on our terms—Jesus/the Holy Spirit intervenes where appropriate—but understand the Bible's meaning here. "Is your life full of difficulties …? Then be happy, for when the way is rough, your patience has a chance to grow" (James 1:2–3 TLB). I am not typically a patient person. I can't tell whether it's my advancing age or directly my growth in the Lord, but I am certainly becoming a more patient person as I mature, both in my natural and spiritual life.

My heart goes out to those who do not believe in anything or anyone beyond this earthly experience. They mock godly people and, in fact, God Himself. They pretend to tease the Holy Spirit, but all they are doing is living a very shallow, surface lifestyle. I once heard a song that wondered about the principles in life. It spoke about the tedious and various faithless events of this world, as the person considers numerous events in his life. The song highlights the behaviors of someone who really had nothing of value to latch onto. Well, I am afraid that for those who subscribe to this ideology, there will come a time when they won't be able to do what they once did anymore, and then I hope they will reach out to God. I know He will take them in, if they ask Him for His saving grace.

Reflection: If you knew the Lord before you began reading this book, or perhaps you prayed the salvation prayer as a result of this reading, you should look to grow your faith. As we've said in this section, there is a process. Challenge the Lord by intentionally turning more and more of your life over to Him. Stay disciplined through study and prayer, and then expect the Holy Spirit to reveal more and more of Himself to you. Be enthusiastic about the outcome as you grow in your walk with God!

JESUS SAYS ...

John 16:7–15

Untypical for this book, all nine verses in this section were spoken by the Lord Jesus Christ. In verse 7, Jesus says, "I tell you the truth ..." (John 16:7 NIV). My first thought was *Yeah, as if Jesus could do anything else!* "I tell you the truth: it is for your good that I am going away" (John 16:7 NIV). Try to imagine being one of the disciples as Jesus attempts to prepare them for His departure from this earth. This kind of reminds me of the old adage with the father, as he is getting ready to physically discipline his son, saying, "Son, this is going to hurt me more than it does you." I can honestly say that I really didn't get spanked very much, and I never recall my father ever giving me that lame speech.

Jesus knew that He would be leaving the world in the hands of His followers. He came to earth as a baby with the distinct purpose of giving Himself up as a sacrifice for our sins—mine and yours! Whenever I think of that, I just cannot fathom the terror that must have driven Jesus to bouts of depression. I haven't specifically read, but certainly we know that Christ came to earth as a human baby, and He experienced all of the same occurrences that any human being could witness and experience. So I don't doubt His being capable of experiencing depression. In the garden of Gethsemane, when He knew He would be arrested, as the disciples accompanying Him continued to fall asleep rather than pray, I am sure Jesus had cause to be disappointed and depressed. I hear depression in his pleadings to them in the Luke account of Jesus before His arrest. Upon reaching the garden at the Mount of Olives, Jesus said, "Pray that you will not fall into temptation" (Luke 22:40 NIV). Jesus also prayed, "Father, if you are willing, take this cup from me; yet not my will, but yours be done" (Luke 22:42 NIV). Can't you hear the agony that Jesus was feeling in that moment?

So what is the takeaway for us *here, right now*? Jesus was One with His Father. He knew why he came down from heaven to earth. *Jesus Christ came down from his Princely position in heaven to die!* And He didn't just die. He died a heinous, criminal, shameful death! I am moved here to reveal that every time I sin, I am going to picture the anguished, hideous-looking Jesus nailed to and hanging on the cross. Do you know why I will do this? I will do this because *it's my fault* that Jesus had to die. Yes, Jesus Christ came down from his Princely position in heaven *to die*—because of *my sin!* Every time I sin, it's like I am asking Christ to go through His agonizing death *all over again*. That is difficult to ponder. I feel the Holy Spirit revealing this image, these words, to my spirit.

Jesus continued. "Unless I go away, the Counselor will not come to you" (John 16:7 NIV). Isn't it just like Jesus to be wanting to leave humankind with someone who will be of Counsel? Lord knows, if we're honest with ourselves, we absolutely need a counselor to stay on track to live a righteous life, in a world where evil seems to be getting more and more pronounced and almost accepted; truth be known, in many circles evil *is* accepted. Higher-order values are not as revered as they once were, even a generation ago. My parents were born in the early 1900s, and my brother and I were raised to believe that *your word is your bond* (not original but valued). I am sorry to say that truth has been slowly watered down with each generation since. When I taught school, I could not just take the word of my students. I needed proof (usually from home) to explain various circumstances. And unfortunately, all too often, the parents were no more honest than their children. (Wow. I wonder how that happened.)

Another term for the Counselor Jesus speaks of is the Holy Spirit. In this book, we have discussed the Holy Spirit. *Being in Step with God* is our book title. Here and now we see where this all happened. How did the Holy Spirit come to us? Jesus tells us in verse 7, "Unless I go away, the Counselor will not come to you" (John 16:7 NIV). So the Holy Spirit came when Jesus left this world. Jesus was human naturally; the Holy Spirit (the Counselor) is *supernatural*. Jesus was limited to being in one place at any given time. Jesus explained, "If I go, I will send him (the Counselor) to you" (John 16:7 NIV). The Holy Spirit can be everywhere at all times! Praise God! Glory to God!

Jesus says, "When [the Holy Spirit] comes, He will convict the world of sin" (John 16:8 NKJV). As we consider the lifestyles of those who traverse the terra firma (that is probably the only scientific term I know), that is those who walk this earth, it becomes quite evident that right from wrong is not clearly differentiated for many. It's not universal. It would seem that their moral compasses do not always point to the truth. Think about it. People cheat on or don't even pay their taxes, they cheat on their spouses (an even more scandalous act), and they lie. "I'm sick today; I can't make it in to work." Worse yet, as an educator, I discovered parents who would cover up their kids' lies with lies of their own—thus compounding the dishonesty. I'm sure that you can add to my list of moral compass imbalances. Well, you know what all this spells, right? S-I-N! "When [the Holy Spirit] comes, He will convict the world of sin" (John 16:8 NKJV) is perhaps a bit more relatable now.

"When [the Holy Spirit] comes, He will convict the world of sin, and of righteousness" (John 16:8 NIV). *Righteousness.* What is it? The dictionary definition is "the quality of being morally right or justifiable" (Google.com/searchrighteousness). My Bible dictionary reads, "Acting in a morally correct manner; correct by divine declaration" (Life Application Study Bible Dictionary/Concordance). At first glance, we might say the two definitions agree. I might argue that to be partially true. The secular dictionary version amuses me a little. "The quality of being morally right or justifiable." Morally right or justifiable—what have we just discussed about society's moral compass? Righteousness according to the world's version is being practiced every day, almost to society's total peril! We have focused on the lack of real truth and overall uprightness, haven't we? Here is where the amusement enters for me: *morally right* or *justifiable*. Don't miss this distinction. Many people go through life *justifying their actions*—self-validating their opinions and behaviors—so that they can live better for themselves. In other words, if they can *justify their actions* for themselves, everything is all right in their world.

Can you see the dilemma our society faces? The secular dictionary version of righteousness gives the populous all the power to decide whether or not their behavior is righteous. Wow! Does that scare you as much as it does me? I am terrified right now. This means that according to the world's definition of righteousness, everybody can decide for themselves what is the right thing to do *morally*. I used to see this all the time when mitigating issues among my students. "Why did you let that boy copy your homework and put his name on it?" The answer: "He said he just didn't have time to do it. He went out and hung around with his friends." What would the righteous thing to do have been for the boy who'd copied instead of doing the work? The answer: take your lumps and hand it in late with a reduced grade. Unfortunately, in the copying student's *justified opinion*, it was no big deal. He could *justify having copied* the other student's work. He had to go out and "hang with his friends." Justified, right?

Now let's look at my Bible dictionary definition. "Acting in a morally correct manner; correct by divine declaration." Notice the distinct difference. We don't read anything about it being "morally right or justifiable." What do we read instead? "Acting in a morally correct manner; correct by divine declaration." We are to be morally correct, and to clarify it for ourselves, "correct" is decided by *divine declaration*. There is no justification on behalf of each individual; God declares whether or not a person is right! Glory to God! Praise God! This takes the mystery out of it. *It takes humankind out of it!*

So how do we know what God wants us to do? There are a couple of ways to accomplish this. We should pray about and listen for the Lord's directions regarding our concerns and read the Bible. "When [the Holy Spirit] comes, He will convict the world of sin, and [explain to the believers about] righteousness" (John 16:8 NKJV). This pretty much wraps this up for us, doesn't it?

There is a bright side to this message from Christ! Jesus wanted to tell the disciples more, but He didn't think they could handle it at the time. I hope you have discovered by now that I continue to try to see the "today relevancy" of the scriptures as I look to apply the scripture verses to my life. I feel that if I am to read it, I should likewise drill down to find how God's Word can be applied to my living. God speaks to us through the history of the life and times of Jesus on this earth 2,000 years ago. The fact that He didn't think they could handle more of what Jesus would have told the believers at the time is encouraging to me. I am better equipped to go to Christ with the events of my life now, because I will be better able to accept Christ's answers, should they be "I have much more to say to you, more than you can bear at this time. But when … the Spirit of truth comes, he will guide you into all truth" (John 16:12–13 NIV). Well, the Spirit *is here*, and He talks to me through prayer and impactful scriptures such as these. So often, while trying to live in this upside-down world, finding the truth is difficult. But I keep coming back to *Being in Step with God*, through the power of the Holy Spirit! The Holy Spirit, when you open up to His leading and guiding, will manage your life for you and reveal the truth in your situations. Isn't that *great news?* Based on the Lord's words in verses 12 and 13, avoid becoming frustrated by having to wait for answers to prayer and other potentially disconcerting events in your life. Be satisfied to wait for the Holy Spirit to lead you to the right answers.

Jesus finished by explaining that

> [the Holy Spirit] will bring glory to [Christ] by taking from what is [Christ's] and making it known to [us]. All that belongs to the Father is [Christ's]. That is why [Jesus] said the Spirit will take from what is [Christ's] and make it known to [us]." (John 16:14–15 NIV)

Reflection: *Being in Step with God* has been all about living according to the leading of the Holy Spirit. *Being in Step with God* talks about surrender, conformity, and discipline. *Surrender* your life to Christ, *conform* to the dictates of Christ, and permit yourself to being *disciplined* by Christ. Can you do this? You cannot do this under your own power, but when you ask God to help you, your life can represent someone as *Being in Step with God.*

Printed in the United States
by Baker & Taylor Publisher Services